CRITIC'S

RECIPE COLLECTION

145 Recipes from
Monterey Peninsula's Best Restaurants

Janice Block

David Rankine

THE CRITIC'S CHOICE

*To the memory of my
brother, Michael Block,
with great love and
appreciation for all he
contributed to me and
everyone else who was
fortunate enough to
have known him.*

Copyright© 1992 by Janice Block

Book and Cover Design by Nina Temple

Typesetting by Instant Type

Published by The Critic's Choice

ISBN 0-9632181-0-7

Printed in the United States of America

First Printing 1992

CONTENTS

■　■　■

ACKNOWLEDGMENTS

■   ■   ■

To the chefs and restaurant owners of the Monterey Peninsula who so generously took time from their busy schedules to provide us with the recipes for this collection. Without their participation, this recipe collection could not of been possible.

To Nina Temple for all her patience and understanding on the long road to finalizing the artwork and illustrations.

To Barbara Kantro and Ticien Carlson for their help in editing and proofreading.

To Kris Martin for all her calculations and formating before she typeset this book.

To Jane Easton for meticulously placing all the logos.

INTRODUCTION

■ ■ ■

Each of the restaurants represented in this recipe collection have all been part of The Critic's Choice Dining Guide of the Monterey Peninsula. The restaurants included in our dining guide are local favorites, based upon the opinion of hundreds of "critics". We interviewed innkeepers, polled local merchants, gathered feedback from diners like yourselves, through surveys and questionnaires, along with our own restaurant experiences over the past 16 years. Each restaurant has been deemed, by popular demand, outstanding for their particular style and cuisine.

After publishing The Critic's Choice Dining Guide for the past 6 years, we felt that introducing this collection of 145 original recipes from the best dining spots on the Monterey Peninsula would offer all of us an inside look at the creative talents of the most celebrated local chefs. From the very traditional preparations to the most novel and contemporary, these easy to follow recipes will allow even the most occasional cook to recreate many of the unique and innovative dishes which have made the restaurants "local" and "international" favorites.

Janice Block   David Rankine

SALAD

VEGETARIAN

ANTON & MICHEL

Tabbouleh

½ cup fine burghul (cracked wheat)
4 bunches parsley, chopped
1 bunch green onions, chopped
2 large tomatoes, diced
½ bunch mint, chopped,
   or 2 Tblsp. dried mint

1 large cucumber,
   peeled and chopped
½ cup olive oil
   juice of 3 lemons
1 Tblsp. salt
½ tsp. pepper
1 head romaine lettuce

■

Wash burghul in cold water and then let it soak for 20 minutes covered with 1″ of water. Drain and squeeze out excess water. Add the burghul to the chopped vegetables and mix all together. Add olive oil, lemon juice, salt and pepper. Allow burghul to soak and absorb the dressing for approximately one hour.
Place the Tabbouleh Salad in a large bowl surrounded with the romaine leaves standing on the edge of the bowl.

Anton
&
Michel

Mission Between Ocean & 7th, Carmel, California
Reservations: 624-2406

■　■　■

Critic's Choice Recipe Collection

BEAU THAI

P'ad Jef Nung
Jef Sax's Special #1

- 1   Tblsp. vegetable oil
- ½ tsp. garlic, chopped
- ½ cup Tofu, firm, cut in ¾" cubes
- 10 cashews, fresh roasted
- 1   cup bamboo shoots, sliced
- ⅓ cup yellow onions, sliced & separated
- ⅓ cup white mushrooms, sliced
- ⅓ cup green onions, cut in 1" pieces
- 4   Chinese snow peas, trimmed
- 4   or 5 pieces broccoli, flowers and sliced stems
- 4   or 5 pieces bell peppers, cut in ¾" squares
- 1   Tblsp. oyster sauce
- ½ cup bean thread noodles, soaked & drained

■

Stir fry for a minute and a half and serve. Serves 2.

DAVID WALTON'S
BEAU THAI
RESTAURANT

807 Cannery Row, Monterey, California
Reservations: 373-8811

■ ■ ■

Critic's Choice Recipe Collection

BINDEL'S

Rock Shrimp and Spinach Salad

1 lb. 2 oz. Rock shrimp
12 oz. baby spinach
1 papaya
4 oz. Macadamia nuts
12 cherry tomatoes
12 cucumbers

Papaya Vinaigrette:
¾ cup fresh papaya puree
¼ cup champagne vinegar
¾ cup walnut oil
salt

■

Arrange cherry tomatoes, which have been cut in half. Place on the outside edge along with sliced cucumbers that have been deseeded. In a bowl mix baby spinach with papaya vinaigrette. Place spinach in center of the plate, arrange slices of papaya on top of spinach. Coarsely chop macadamia nuts and sprinkle on top. Just before serving saute rock shrimp and spoon on top of spinach.

Papaya Vinaigrette: Place papaya puree in a mixing bowl, whip in champagne vinegar. Slowly add walnut oil while continuing to whip. Season with Kosher salt. Depending on sweetness of papaya, add a pinch of sugar. Serves 6.

Bindel's

500 Hartnell, Monterey, California
Reservations: 373-3737

■ ■ ■

Critic's Choice Recipe Collection

CENTRAL 159

Fresh or Wilted Spinach Salad Dressing

12 cloves garlic, peeled
1½ Tblsp. dijon mustard
 1 cup sherry vinegar
 3 cups olive or peanut oil

■

Place garlic, mustard, and vinegar in bowl of food processor or blender with the cutting blade. Process until the garlic is completely chopped. With the processor running, slowly drizzle in oil continuously until dressing is completely emulsified. Refrigerate until ready to serve.
Either hot or cold, use approximately 3 Tblsp. of dressing per serving.
Yield: 1 quart.

159 Central Avenue, Pacific Grove, California
Reservations: 372-2235

■   ■   ■

Critic's Choice Recipe Collection

CLUB XIX

Nectarine, Green Bean and Avocado Salad

2 each nectarines (ripe)
6 oz. green beans (medium Blue Lake)
1 avocado
½ bunch tarragon (finely minced)
¼ cup tarragon vinegar
1 cup walnut oil
3 Tblsp. Kosher salt
½ cup toasted almonds

■

Peel and seed nectarine and avocado. Cut each lengthwise and slice ¼″ thick.
Transfer ingredients to bowl and pour tarragon vinegar and minced tarragon over
mixture. Reserve.
Blanch green beans in salted boiling water for 2 minutes. Strain and shock beans in
ice water. Remove green beans from ice and pat dry. Combine all ingredients and
mix thoroughly. Let salad marinate 1 hour before serving. Serves 6.

C   L   U   B   ˇ

XIX

The Lodge at Pebble Beach, 17 Mile Drive
Reservations: 624-3811

■   ■   ■

Critic's Choice Recipe Collection

CYPRESS ROOM

Warm Spinach Salad
with Pancetta, Shitake Mushrooms and Walnuts

8 oz. spinach, well washed and destemmed
3 oz. Pancetta bacon, in ¼" cubes
3 bulbs garlic - crushed & diced
¼ oz. Balsamic vinegar
1 oz. apple cider vinegar
1 oz. rice wine vinegar
1 tsp. olive oil
1 tsp. sugar
4 oz. walnut pieces
3 each Shitake mushrooms, sliced
1 6" saute pan
  mixing bowl

■

Heat saute pan, add Pancetta and cook until lightly brown, add garlic and brown, add rest of ingredients, except walnuts and spinach. Let simmer 5 minutes and remove from heat and put in mixing bowl. Add spinach and toss until lightly wilted. Sprinkle walnuts over the salad and serve immediately. This salad has to be served warm. Serves 2.

THE CYPRESS ROOM

The Lodge at Pebble Beach, 17 Mile Drive
Reservations: 624-3811

■ ■ ■

Critic's Choice Recipe Collection

DELFINO'S ON THE BAY

Fresh Mushroom Salad
with Lemon and Leeks

1 lb. regular white mushrooms
   juice of 2 lemons
1 leek
2 oz. extra virgin olive oil
   salt
   black pepper
1 head butter lettuce

■

Slice mushrooms and leek very thin and place in bowl. Mix lemon juice, extra virgin olive oil, salt with a whisk and pour over mushrooms and leeks. Mix well and put on plates covered with butter lettuce leaves. Serves 4.

Monterey Plaza Hotel, 400 Cannery Row, Monterey, California
Reservations: 646-1706

■   ■   ■

Critic's Choice Recipe Collection

DIÁNA

Brandade of Celery Root and Fennel

1 medium celery root (approx. 1½ lbs.)
  peeled and quartered
2 fennel bulbs (1½ lbs.)
  trimmed and quartered
2 large white fleshed potatoes (1 lb.)
  peeled and quartered
1 lemon, juiced
4 cloves garlic

⅓ cup olive oil
2 cups heavy cream
1 star anise
  salt and pepper to taste
2 Tblsp. parsley, chopped
4 slices fine textured white
  bread, halved diagonally

■

Place celery root, fennel and potatoes in steamer. Sprinkle with half lemon juice and steam until tender. Drain well.

Meanwhile in small skillet, saute garlic in the olive oil on low heat for 3 minutes. Do not let brown. Heat cream in a small saucepan over low heat for 3-5 minutes. Grind star anise to a fine powder.

Place steamed vegetables in food processor. Set aside 1 Tblsp. of oil used for garlic. Turn processor on. Slowly add hot olive oil and garlic until smooth and creamy, about 1 minute. Pour puree into a large mixing bowl. Add hot cream, anise, salt and pepper, remaining lemon juice and blend well.

Heat reserved olive oil in small skillet. Add bread and quickly brown on both sides. Drain croutons on paper towels. Place puree in heat proof serving dish and smooth. Sprinkle with parsley. Place croutons on top. Serve hot. Serves 4.

DIÁNA

Carmel Plaza, Ocean & Junipero, Carmel, California
Reservations: 626-0191

■ ■ ■

Critic's Choice Recipe Collection

EL COCODRILO

Black Beans Otomi

1 lb. black beans, washed and drained
1 onion, chopped
¼ cup oil
5 cloves garlic, minced
2 serrano chiles (small green chiles)
2 quarts rich vegetable or chicken stock
   (the richer the better)
1 tsp. salt & pepper (or more to taste)

■

Make sure the beans are thoroughly cleaned. Add beans, onion, oil, garlic and chiles to stock. Use a heavy stock pot (or clay pot if you have one). Bring to a boil. Then reduce to simmer for 5 hours, stirring occasionally, on a very low heat. The beans will become soft and the longer they are cooked, the thicker and richer the stock will become. Add a little more liquid if necessary, but don't let the beans burn on the bottom! Serve with sour cream (or creme fraiche) and a sprig of cilantro. Serves 6.

El Cocodrilo

ROTISSERIE and SEAFOOD GRILL

701 Lighthouse Avenue, Pacific Grove, California
Reservations: 655-3311

■   ■   ■

Critic's Choice Recipe Collection

FANDANGO

Salade Nicoise

1 head butter lettuce or red lettuce, washed and drained
2 medium tomatoes, quartered
⅓ green bell pepper, cut in ¼" strips
⅓ sweet yellow pepper, cut in ¼" strips
⅓ sweet red bell pepper, cut in ¼" strips
1 heart of celery, diced
½ cucumber, peeled and sliced
3 green onions, chopped
1 medium potato, boiled and diced in ½" cubes

1 cup cooked string beans
1 cup canned tuna, drained (preferably water packed)
9 anchovy fillets
½ cup Nicoise olives (tiny black olives packed in brine, not oil)
3 hard boiled eggs, quartered lengthwise
several fresh basil leaves, chopped
vinaigrette*

■

Arrange lettuce around a salad bowl. Place tomato quarters on top of lettuce leaves. Combine bell peppers, celery, cucumber, potatoes and green beans and arrange decoratively on top of tomatoes. Sprinkle the tuna and chopped basil on top of vegetables. Top each salad with 1-2 anchovy fillets, 2 egg quarters, a few olives and green onions. Dress the salad with vinaigrette immediately before serving and toss lightly. Serves 6.

*When preparing the vinaigrette, use less vinegar and more mustard than usually required.

fandango

223 17th Street, Pacific Grove, California
Reservations: 372-3456

■   ■   ■

Critic's Choice Recipe Collection

FIFI'S CAFE & BAKERY

Stir-Fried Vegetables
with Garlic

2 Tblsp. sherry
1 Tblsp. soy sauce
1 cup chicken broth
1 tsp. sugar
2 Tblsp. cornstarch
4 cups fresh vegetables,
   cut in even bite size pieces
1 tsp. oil to stir-fry
2 or 3 cloves garlic, chopped fine
1 tsp. fresh ginger, grated (optional)

■

Mix the sherry, soy, chicken broth, sugar and cornstarch. Set aside. Heat the wok on high heat with about 1 tsp. oil. Add the vegetables and fry while stirring. You can stir-fry one vegetable at a time or start with the one that takes the longest and then add the others. Add water as you need it, a little at a time. Remove the vegetables and add just a drop of oil. Add the garlic and then add the ginger (if you choose). Fry for a few seconds and then add the chicken broth mixture. Bring to a boil and cook until clear. Then return the vegetables to the pan. Serve as soon as possible. Serve with ¾ cup rice with each portion. Serves 2.

Fifi's Cafe
& BAKERY

1188 Forest Avenue, Pacific Grove, California
Reservations: 372-5235

■ ■ ■

Critic's Choice Recipe Collection

FISHWIFE AT ASILOMAR BEACH

Salsa Brava

½ head white cabbage
½ medium onion, diced
½ green bell pepper, diced
½ red bell pepper, diced
4 Serrano chiles, finely chopped*
1 tsp. salt
⅛ Tblsp. black pepper

Dressing:
1 cup white vinegar
½ Tblsp. sugar
⅛ Tblsp. salt

■

Combine the vegetables, ¼ tsp. salt and the black pepper in a large mixing bowl. Stir in the dressing of vinegar, sugar and ⅛ Tblsp. salt. Pack the Salsa Brava in a lidded container for at least 8 hours before serving to allow the cabbage to "Pickle". Salsa Brava will keep for a good week in the refrigerator so it's a great make-ahead dish. Serves 8 portions.

*Adjust number to taste.
Note: This is a condiment used with seafood and fried dishes.

1996 Sunset Drive, Pacific Grove, California
Reservations: 375-7107

■   ■   ■

Critic's Choice Recipe Collection

FRESH CREAM

Vegetarian Souffle

¼ cup milk
¼ cup flour
¼ tsp. salt and white pepper
¼ cup milk, scalded
5 egg yolks (reserve whites for later)
1 Tblsp. butter
2 Tblsp. lemon juice
½ cup vegetables
2 Tblsp. nuts
2 Tblsp. cheese
2 egg whites per 5 oz. souffle

■

In bowl over double boiler whisk milk, flour, salt and pepper. Stir often until thick paste has formed. Add scalded milk, stir until paste has same thickness. Remove from heat, add egg yolks, butter and lemon juice. Cool.
Grease and flour souffle cups.
Whip 2 egg whites until rising mixture begins to receed. Combine egg whites with 2 Tblsp. of souffle paste, fold in vegetables, nuts and cheese. Overfill souffle cup without spilling.
Bake at 400° for 5-7 minutes or until golden brown. Serves 1, 5 oz. souffle.

100 F Heritage Harbor, Monterey, California
Reservations: 375-9798

■　■　■

Critic's Choice Recipe Collection

GERNOT'S VICTORIA HOUSE

Champignons Frits

½ lb. fresh mushrooms
½ cup flour
2 eggs, beaten
1 cup bread crumbs, white French bread
2 cups oil
  tartar sauce
  lemon wedge as garnish

Tartar Sauce:
½ cup mayonnaise
1 dill pickle, chopped
  chopped chives
  onion or green onions
  pickle juice as needed

■

Wash and quarter mushrooms. Bread them by dipping first in flour, in egg, then breadcrumbs. Fry mushrooms in hot oil until golden brown. Scoop out mushrooms with a strainer, letting excess oil drip off. Salt lightly. Serve with tartar sauce and lemon wedge.

Tartar Sauce: Mix all ingredients into the mayonnaise. If mixture seems too thick, add a little pickle juice or vinegar. Serves 4.

649 Lighthouse Avenue, Pacific Grove, California
Reservations: 646-1477

■ ■ ■

Critic's Choice Recipe Collection

GREAT WALL

Chinese Chicken Salad

½ lb. filet of chicken breast,
   lean and skinned
¼ head iceburg lettuce, shredded
¼ cup carrots, shredded
1 cup crispy Chinese rice noodles
1 Tblsp. green onion,
   green part sliced small

Dressing:
1 Tblsp. ground crunchy peanuts
1 tsp. hot Chinese yellow mustard
½ tsp. white vinegar
½ tsp. sesame oil
⅛ tsp. salt
⅛ tsp. sugar
⅛ tsp. white pepper

Coat chicken breast with flour. Cook in corn oil for ten minutes until crispy. After it is cooked, cut into strips. Place into big bowl.

Dressing: Mix all ingredients and toss with cooked chicken. Garnish with toasted sesame seeds. Serves 1.

長 城

GREAT WALL
CHINESE RESTAURANT

731 A Munras Avenue, Monterey, California
Reservations: 372-3637

■   ■   ■

Critic's Choice Recipe Collection

HIGHLANDS INN

Watercress Pear Salad

2 bunches watercress, washed,
   large stems removed
1 ripe but firm pear,
   quartered, cored, thin sliced
4 oz. roquefort cheese
4 oz. fresh chestnuts
   (if unavailable, pecans or walnuts)
4 oz. red wine vinaigrette

■

Lightly toss watercress, pear slices, cheese with vinaigrette. Arrange on four salad plates. Heat nuts for one minute in 350° oven, sprinkle over salad. Serves 4.

HIGHLANDS INN

Four Miles South of Carmel on Highway One, Carmel, California
Reservations: 624-3801

■ ■ ■

Critic's Choice Recipe Collection

KIEWEL'S

Vegetarian Garden Sandwich

8 slices 9 grain bread
1 cucumber, sliced
1 tomato, sliced
4 leaves green leaf lettuce
   washed and dried
1 avocado, peeled and sliced
4 oz. cream cheese, softened (optional)

■

Spread softened cream cheese on bread slices. Place lettuce, tomato, cucumber, and avocado evenly on bread. Top with remaining slices of bread, slice and serve. Serves 4.

100 A Heritage Harbor, Monterey, California
Reservations: 372-6950

■ ■ ■

Critic's Choice Recipe Collection

LA BRASSERIE "Q" POINT

Heart of Romaine Salad
with Almonds and Gorgonzola Dressing

1 bunch Romaine lettuce	**Gorgonzola Dressing:**
1 oz. toasted almonds	6 oz. Gorgonzola cheese
1 oz. croutons	9 oz. extra virgin olive oil
3 oz. sliced tomatoes	3 oz. salad oil
1 Tblsp. parsley	2 oz. white wine vinegar
1 oz. domestic Gorgonzola cheese	juice from ½ lemon
	pinch salt & pepper

■

Dressing: Mix cheese, extra virgin olive oil, salad oil, white wine vinegar, lemon juice, salt and pepper in a blender.

Salad: Arrange Romaine lettuce on plate and top with croutons, almonds, tomatoes, and parsley, crumble 1 oz. of Gorgonzola cheese over salad and add dressing. Serves 2.

La Brasserie
QPoint
of Carmel

Ocean between Dolores & Lincoln, Carmel, California
Reservations: 624-2569

■ ■ ■

Critic's Choice Recipe Collection

LOS LAURELES RESTAURANT

Gazpacho

20 ripe Roma tomatoes
 2 red onions
 1 red bell pepper
 1 yellow bell pepper
 1 cucumber (peeled & seeded)
 3 sprigs tarragon
¼ bunch basil
¼ bunch cilantro
 1 Tblsp. sesame oil
 8 Tblsp. olive oil (extra virgin)
 1 can tomato juice
    salt & fresh white pepper
 1 dash tabasco

■

Take above items and pass through meat grinder on large setting. Season and chill. Garnish with fine diced cucumbers, chive stems, & lime wheel.

LOS LAURELES

313 West Carmel Valley Road, Carmel, California
Reservations: 659-2233

■ ■ ■

Critic's Choice Recipe Collection

MONTEREY JOE'S

Penne Con Pepperoni

1   lb. Roma tomatoes
1   red bell pepper
1   green bell pepper
½ Bermuda onion
15 small Calmalta olives
2   Tblsp. capers
2   tsp. pine nuts
2   cloves garlic
2   sprigs basil
16 oz. penne pasta

■

Cook the red and green bell pepper, onion, olives, capers, and pine nuts in olive oil, without browning. Add to a puree of tomatoes, garlic, and basil. Serve on penne pasta. Serves 4.

2149 North Fremont, Monterey, California
Reservations: 655-3355

■   ■   ■

Critic's Choice Recipe Collection

OLD BATH HOUSE

Avocado and Grilled Artichoke Heart Salad

9 oz. mixed baby greens
3 avocados
12 artichoke hearts
6 red cherry tomatoes
6 yellow pear tomatoes
½ cucumber
1 pear, sliced

Pear and Hazelnut Dressing:
½ pear
1 cup hazelnut oil
½ cup pear vinegar
⅛ cup shallots, chopped
salt and white pepper

■

Cook artichokes in boiling water with 1 lemon cut in half and 2 whole cloves, approximately 20-25 minutes or until tender. Cool off in ice water. Grill at service time.

Cut tomatoes in half and arrange on outside edge of plate along with deseeded and sliced cucumbers. Place greens in center of plate. Take avocado out and remove the seed. Cut each ½ in 4 sections. Arrange on top of greens. Place sliced pears on greens. Cut grilled artichoke hearts in ½, arrange on greens. Top with pear and hazelnut dressing.

Pear and Hazelnut Dressing: Peel and take out core of pear. Cut into small cubes. Place in bowl. Add vinegar & shallots slowly. Add hazelnut oil, whip and season with Kosher salt and freshly grated white pepper. Serves 6.

Old Bath House
R E S T A U R A N T

620 Oceanview Boulevard, Pacific Grove, California
Reservations: 375-5195

■   ■   ■

Critic's Choice Recipe Collection

PEPPERS MEXICALI CAFE

Grilled Sea Scallop Salad
with Cilantro Vinaigrette

1 lb. fresh sea scallops
1 each red leaf,
   romaine and butter lettuce
3 sliced tomatoes
   black olives, pitted
3 scallions

Vinaigrette:
2 Tblsp. white wine
2 Tblsp. orange juice
2 Tblsp. fresh lime juice
2 Tblsp. rice wine vinegar
6 Tblsp. olive oil
½ cup chopped cilantro
   pinch of salt, pepper & sugar
1 clove garlic, minced

■

Combine all ingredients for the vinaigrette and mix well. Toss cleaned lettuce, torn into bite-sized pieces with the vinaigrette.
Grill or broil scallops until they are opaque in the center.
Garnish lettuce with tomatoes, olives, scallions and top with warm grilled scallops.
Serves 6.

170 Forest Avenue, Pacific Grove, California
Reservations: 373-6892

■   ■   ■

Critic's Choice Recipe Collection

RIO GRILL

Watercress, Orange Lemon Salad

4 oranges	**Black Pepper Citrus Vinaigrette:**
4 lemons	1 cup mild olive oil
12 cherry tomatoes	½ cup fresh orange juice
3 oz. blue cheese, crumbled	¼ cup fresh lemon juice
¼ cup walnuts, toasted	2 Tblsp. coarsely ground pepper
	salt to taste

■

Cut the peel and all the white pith from the oranges and lemons. Cut crosswise into ¼" thick slices and remove seeds.

Toss watercress, walnuts, and cherry tomatoes with half of vinaigrette. Arrange watercress on 6 chilled salad plates. Arrange tomatoes, walnuts, lemon and orange throughout salad. Drizzle remaining vinaigrette over salad and top with blue cheese. Serves 6.

Highway One & Rio Road, Carmel, California
Reservations: 625-5436

■ ■ ■

Critic's Choice Recipe Collection

SANDBAR & GRILL

Veggie Eggs Benedict

4 eggs, poached
2 English muffins
    Hollandaise sauce
2 cups total of diced mushrooms, artichoke
    hearts, tomatoes, and bell pepper
1 avocado, sliced

■

Grill all vegetables lightly. Toast muffins with butter. Top muffins with vegetables,
evenly. Top with poached egg, Hollandaise, and avocado. Serve with hash browns.
Serves 2.

Wharf #2, Monterey, California
Information: 373-2818

■   ■   ■

Critic's Choice Recipe Collection

SANS SOUCI

Salad Tomates Aux Basilque
Tomato Basil Salad

4 large ripe tomatoes
1 Tblsp. minced fresh basil
3 Tblsp. olive oil
1 Tblsp. lemon juice
   salt & cracked black pepper
⅛ lb. Feta cheese, crumbled (optional)

■

Arrange slices of tomatoes on 4 plates. Mix lemon juice, olive oil & basil in a bowl.
Pour equally over sliced tomatoes, salt & pepper, top with crumbled Feta. Serves 4.

Sans Souci

French Cuisine

Lincoln between 5th & 6th, Carmel, California
Reservations: 624-6220

■   ■   ■

Critic's Choice Recipe Collection

SPADARO'S RISTORANTE

Melanzanie Al Formagio
Stuffed Eggplant

   1 whole eggplant
6-8 whole Italian pear tomatoes, fresh or canned
   ¼ lb. smoked Gouda cheese, grated
   ½ lb. imported Goat cheese, grated
   3 cloves garlic, chopped
   1 bunch fresh basil, chopped
   5 Tblsp. olive oil
      salt and pepper, to taste

■

Slice eggplant ¼" thick. Heat medium sauce pan with 4 Tblsp. olive oil. Place eggplant slices in heated oil. Cook until slices are brown on each side. Then place cooked slices on towel to absorb excess oil. Place grated Goat and Gouda cheese on each slice and then roll each slice up with the cheese in the middle. Place all rolled slices on a sheet pan until the cheese melts. Serve with sauce.

Sauce: Saute garlic in 1 Tblsp. olive oil until browned. Add tomatoes to the pan. If you are using canned tomatoes, smash whole tomatoes with hand. If you are using fresh tomatoes, dice with knife. Simmer for 10 minutes. Add basil, salt and pepper. Place eggplant on plate and top with sauce. Serves 4.

Spadaro's
RISTORANTE

650 Cannery Row, Monterey, California
Reservations: 372-8881

■ ■ ■

Critic's Choice Recipe Collection

TASTE CAFE & BISTRO

Mediterranean Chicken Salad

Dressing:
7 oz. Feta cheese
1½ oz. blue cheese
4 oz. cream cheese, softened
¾ cup sour cream
½ cup plain yogurt
½ Tblsp. fresh tarragon, finely chopped
½ Tblsp. fresh basil, chopped
   salt
   fresh ground white pepper

Salad:
5 heads Romaine, cut into pieces
4 2½ lb. roasted chickens-skinned, boned and cut into pieces or 10 chicken breasts— poached and cut into pieces
3 English cucumbers, sliced
10 cherry tomatoes, halved
1 medium red onion, halved, thinly sliced
40 Kalamata olives
2 red bell peppers, roasted, peeled and cut into strips

■

Dressing: Using blender or food processor fitted with steel blade, blend the cheeses, sour cream, yogurt, salt and pepper for one minute. The puree should not be completely smooth, but should have some texture. Stir in tarragon and basil.

Salad: Toss Romaine with salad dressing and arrange on plates. Garnish with chicken pieces, cucumbers, onions, Kalamata olives, tomato halves and red pepper strips. Drizzle more dressing on top of chicken and sprinkle with freshly chopped Italian parsley. Serves 10.

TaSte
CAFE & BISTRO

1199 Forest Avenue, Pacific Grove, California
Reservations: 655-0324

■ ■ ■

Critic's Choice Recipe Collection

THE FABULOUS TOOT'S LAGOON

Sauteed Mushroom Appetizer

½ lb. medium mushrooms
½ lemon
1   clove garlic, crushed
2   oz. white wine
2   oz. butter
1   bay leaf
½ tsp. salt
1   Tblsp. peanut oil

■

In a hot saute pan add peanut oil and heat until hot. Add mushrooms and quickly brown them. Add garlic and squeeze juice from the ½ lemon. Then add bay leaf, white wine, and salt. Simmer for about 2 minutes, then add butter and reduce for about two more minutes. Serves 2.

Dolores between Ocean & 7th, Carmel, California
Reservations: 625-1915

■   ■   ■

Critic's Choice Recipe Collection

THE TINNERY

Bay Shrimp Salad

1   lb. bay shrimp (cooked)
½ lb. spinach, cleaned
1   cup artichoke hearts
1   cup diced tomatoes
½ cup cucumbers, chopped
¼ cup olive oil
¼ cup celery, chopped
⅕ cup red wine vinegar
⅓ tsp. oregano

■

Mix together and serve on platter. Serves 4.

631 Oceanview Boulevard, Pacific Grove, California
Reservations: 646-1040

■   ■   ■

Critic's Choice Recipe Collection

SEAFOOD

ANTON & MICHEL

Sauteed Abalone Medallions

1 lb. cultured Abalone medallions
   (2½" - 3½")
1 cup corn flour or white flour
1 cup butter or margarine
¼ cup lemon juice, (or half lemon juice,
   half white wine)

■

If abalone is frozen, make sure it is thoroughly thawed before separating the
medallions to avoid tearing. If abalone if fresh, remove from container and discard
the liquid.
Lightly dust the abalone medallions on both sides with flour. Melt butter in a sauce
pan. Heat a large heavy gauge frying pan. Pour half cup of butter into the frying
pan and heat until butter sizzles. Place abalone medallions to cover the bottom of
the pan. Cook each side on high heat for 30 seconds and add half of the lemon juice
during the cooking. Remove from pan and keep warm. Repeat the above procedure
until all medallions are cooked. Serve immediately after cooking. Serves 4.

**Anton
&
Michel**

Mission between Ocean & 7th, Carmel, California
Reservations: 624-2406

■ ■ ■

Critic's Choice Recipe Collection

BEAU THAI

Plakapong Daeng P'Ad P'Rig

½ cup vegetable oil
2 2″ x 3″ pieces rock cod filet, lightly floured
1 Tblsp. vegetable oil
½ tsp. garlic, chopped
3 small squirts fish sauce
⅓ cup red chili paste
½ tsp. curry powder, Madras light
⅓ cup ginger, peeled & cut in small strips
1 cup bamboo shoots, sliced
12 pieces kaffir lime leaf, threaded
⅓ cup green onions, cut in 1″ pieces
⅓ cup yellow onions, sliced & separated
4–5 pieces bell peppers, cut in ¾″ squares

■

Deep fry cod in ½ cup oil until it has a crisp surface. Add remaining ingredients in another pan. Add fish & stir fry. Add soup stock to moisten sauce, stir fry and serve. Serves 2.

DAVID WALTON'S
BEAU THAI
RESTAURANT

807 Cannery Row, Monterey, California
Reservations: 373-8811

■   ■   ■

Critic's Choice Recipe Collection

BINDEL'S

Red Snapper
with Tomato Avocado Salsa

2½ lb. red snapper, 7 oz. portions
4 oz. black beans
1 serrano pepper, chopped
2 oz. Myers rum
½ oz. white onion, diced
2 strips bacon, diced
   chicken stock
½ pint heavy cream
   kosher salt

Tomato Avocado Salsa:
1 lb. roma tomatoes
¼ white onion, diced
1 lime
¼ bunch cilantro
1½ avocados
   salt and pepper
   pinch of fresh oregano
2 serranos

■

Snapper: Make sure all bones are removed from fish. Dredge in flour that has cayenne pepper in it. Melt butter in saute pan. When lightly brown, place fish in and brown. Turn over, cook in oven at 350° for 10 minutes. Place snapper on the black bean sauce and top with tomato avocado salsa. Serves 6.

Black Bean Sauce: Soak black beans overnight. Strain. Lightly brown bacon, add white onions, cook until tender. Add black beans, serrano, Myers rum, cover with chicken stock. Season with salt. When beans are very soft add ½ pint heavy cream and ½ pint chicken stock. Reduce a little then blenderize. If too thick, add a little chicken stock to thin out.

Tomato Avocado Salsa: Take seeds out of tomatoes and cut in ¼ inch cubes. Dice onions, split serranos in ½ lengthwise and slice; chop oregano and cilantro. Cut avocados and cube. Add juice from 1 lime, mix and season with salt and pepper.

Bindel's

500 Hartnell, Monterey, California
Reservations: 373-3737

■　■　■

Critic's Choice Recipe Collection

CENTRAL 159

Zesty Summer Grilled Fish Marinade

1   roasted, peeled and seeded jalapeno chili
2   cloves finely chopped or slivered garlic
1   bunch cilantro, completely stemmed
    (leaves only)
3   lemons, zest and juice
1   soaked dry annahiem or ancho chili pod
1   bunch scallions
2   cups peanut or olive oil (to cover only)
6   peeled shallots, coarsely chopped

■

In a low pan or medium mixing bowl, place chopped garlic and the peeled and seeded jalapeno. To this add the coarsely chopped cilantro and lemon juice with the chopped zest. Add diced scallions and shallots. Cut the ancho into long strips and add into the mixture and toss. Add 1 cup of oil and pour over the fish of your choice. Add remaining oil only if necessary to evenly coat all fish filets. Serves 6. **CAUTION:** Do not float the fish in the marinade. This will only dilute the flavors.

159 Central Avenue, Pacific Grove, California
Reservations: 372-2235

■   ■   ■

Critic's Choice Recipe Collection

CLUB XIX

Monterey Spot Prawns
and Roma Tomato Confit

18 large Spot Prawns, cleaned and deveined
 3 oz. white wine
 6 oz. heavy cream
 2 oz. whole grain mustard
12 roma tomatoes
 3 oz. olive oil
 1 bunch tarragon
 1 oz. garlic, minced
 3 oz. butter, unsalted
   zest of 1 lemon, blanched
   salt and pepper to taste

■

Tomato Confit: Cut the end off the tomatoes and gently squeeze out the seeds. Coat the tomatoes with olive oil and cook in 250° oven for one hour. Peel and coarsely chop the tomatoes. Set aside.

Cooking process: In a large saute pan combine the garlic, white wine and whole grain mustard. Bring to a boil and reduce the volume by half. Add the prawns and cream and slowly simmer four minutes. Next add the tomato confit, tarragon and lemon zest and simmer for two minutes. Remove pan from the flame and whisk the butter into the mixture. Salt and pepper to taste, serve immediately. Serves 6.

At Club XIX, this dish is served with angel hair pasta, a grilled half of Roma tomato drizzled with olive oil, and a sprig of tarragon.

C   L   U   B

XIX

The Lodge at Pebble Beach, 17 Mile Drive
Reservations: 624-3811

■   ■   ■

Critic's Choice Recipe Collection

CYPRESS ROOM

Seared Scallops
with Angel Hair Pasta, Corn Relish & Citrus Glaze

20 sea scallops
  Flour for dredging
4 oz. clarified butter
8 oz. cooked angel
  hair pasta
6 oz. whole butter
12 oz. corn relish
6 oz. orange juice
2 whole jalapeno
  peppers (garnish)
3 Saute pans, 2 - 6", 1 - 10"

Corn Relish:
9 oz. kernel corn
3 oz. diced red and green
  bell peppers
1 sliced green onion
  White pepper to taste
¼ oz. sugar

■

Corn Relish: Mix all ingredients together.

Scallops: In a 10" saute pan heat clarified butter, dredge scallops in flour and sear in butter until golden brown and cooked. Remove from pan and discard remaining butter. Deglaze pan with orange juice and let reduce until juice starts to glaze in pan. Add 2 oz. whole butter and stir to mix with orange juice. Put glaze on each scallop on plate.
In other 2 pans, heat 2 oz. whole butter and add relish. Saute until hot. Heat last 2 oz. of butter in pan, add pasta and season to taste.
Arrange the pasta as a roll (nest) in the center of the plate. Place the scallops around the pasta alternating with the relish to achieve a nice plate presentation. Serves 4.

THE CYPRESS ROOM ˙

The Lodge at Pebble Beach, 17 Mile Drive
Reservations: 624-3811

■   ■   ■

Critic's Choice Recipe Collection

DELFINO'S ON THE BAY

BBQ'd Swordfish
with Fresh Tomatoes, Garlic Capers and Extra Virgin Olive Oil

- 4 swordfish steaks (approx. 7 oz. ea.)
- 4 roma tomatoes
- 1 oz. minced garlic
- 2 Tblsp. capers
- 2 oz. extra virgin olive oil
- 2 fl. oz. dry white wine
  salt, black pepper (peppermill)

■

Trim the dark portion of the swordfish and remove skin. Brush lightly with olive oil and season with salt and black pepper. Place on hot BBQ or grill. Cook steaks for approx. 4 minutes on each side depending on thickness of steaks (do not overcook swordfish or it could get very dry).

Cut tomatoes in ¼ inch cubes. Saute the tomatoes, garlic and capers in the extra virgin olive oil. Do not add the wine until the juice from the tomatoes is completely reduced. Add the wine and cook the sauce over high heat while stirring the sauce constantly. Season with fresh ground pepper. Salt is usually not necessary because of the zestyness of the capers.

Divide the sauce on four plates and place the swordfish on top. Serve with rice and grilled vegetables. Serves 4.

Monterey Plaza Hotel, 400 Cannery Row, Monterey, California
Reservations: 646-1706

■　■　■

Critic's Choice Recipe Collection

DIÁNA

Sole

 1 lb. filet of sole
 1 cup flour
½ cup virgin olive oil
¼ cup white wine
16 snow peas, julienned
 2 sprigs watercress
 2 lemons
    salt & pepper to taste

■
Salt and pepper filets. Lightly flour filets. Heat teflon pan, pour in ¼ cup oil and saute sole until golden brown on both sides. Remove from pan and squeeze lemon into pan. Add white wine, snow peas, watercress and remaining olive oil. Swirl in the pan and pour over the fish. Serve with rice and vegetables. Serves 4.

DIÁNA

Carmel Plaza, Ocean & Junipero, Carmel, California
Reservations: 626-0191

■   ■   ■

Critic's Choice Recipe Collection

EL COCODRILO

Prawns Belize

42 large prawns,
   peeled and deveined
   flour
5 ripe tomatoes
1 red (Bermuda) onion
1 bunch cilantro
6 limes
1 medium jicama
   (about the size of an orange)
5 serrano chiles
   (small green)
2 oz. white wine
   handful roasted cashew nuts
   salt and pepper to taste

■

Salsa: Dice tomatoes, onion, jicama; mince chiles; chop cilantro. Mix together.
Squeeze limes and add their juice. Correct seasoning with salt and pepper.

Prawns: Lightly flour prawns. Divide into two groups: either cook them
simultaneously in 2 pans, or sequentially in 2 batches. This is to insure proper
cooking.
To frying pan, add enough oil (preferably peanut) to cover bottom. Heat until the oil
is almost smoking. NEVER LET THE OIL SMOKE. Add prawns and toss until
cooked (curly and pink). If the prawns get dry, add more oil. When almost done,
add wine—this will finish the cooking. Add half the salsa (the other half is for the
second batch of prawns). Cook until the salsa is heated.
Top dish with chopped cilantro and the cashew nuts. Serve with salad, rice and
black beans. Serves 6.

El Cocodrilo

ROTISSERIE and SEAFOOD GRILL

701 Lighthouse Avenue, Pacific Grove, California
Reservations: 655-3311

■ ■ ■

Critic's Choice Recipe Collection

FANDANGO

Scampi Basquaise

24 to 32 prawns (16-20 count per lb.),
   shelled, deveined
4 shallots, chopped
1 large ripe tomato, diced
4 bunches spinach leaves, destemmed
1 jigger cognac
½ cup fresh green peas
5 oz. white wine
½ oz. raspberry vinegar
   olive oil, butter, salt, pepper
   cayenne pepper, to taste

■

Heat olive oil and butter in skillet; add prawns and saute briefly. Add shallots, cognac and flambe'. Add sliced tomatoes, peas, white wine, and spinach leaves. Reduce to low heat for a few minutes, sprinkle on raspberry vinegar, season with salt, pepper, and cayenne. Serve over saffron rice or spaghettini. Serves 4.

fandango

223 17th Street, Pacific Grove, California
Reservations: 372-3456

■   ■   ■

Critic's Choice Recipe Collection

FIFI'S CAFE & BAKERY

Filet of Sole
with Fresh Tarragon or Fresh Basil

⅓ lb. petrale sole filets
4 Tblsp. olive oil
4 Tblsp. lemon juice
8 Tblsp. white wine
2 Tblsp. chopped fresh parsley
2 Tblsp. fresh tarragon or basil, chopped
   salt and pepper to taste

■

Place the sole snugly into a baking dish. Mix the remaining ingredients. Pour over the fish. Bake, covered for about 20 minutes, until the sole is opaque and firm. Baste with the juices on the bottom of the pan after 10 minutes. Low calorie recipe. Serves 4.

Fifi's Cafe
& BAKERY

1188 Forest Ave., Pacific Grove, California
Reservations: 372-5235

■   ■   ■

Critic's Choice Recipe Collection

FISHWIFE AT ASILOMAR BEACH

Cajun Snapper

4 7-8 oz. fresh snapper filets (no bones)
2 Tblsp. paprika
1 tsp. cayenne pepper
1 tsp. salt
½ tsp. white pepper
½ tsp. onion powder
1 tsp. garlic powder
¼ tsp. dry dill
2 Tblsp. peanut oil

■

Dry fish filets with a towel. Place the herbs and spices in a paper bag. Coat the filets with the cajun spice mixture by shaking them, one by one, in the bag.

Cook the filets on a grill at 350° for 5 minutes on the first side, and 3 minutes on the second side. (Or, pan fry in 2 Tblsp. peanut oil: put the fish in the pan before the oil smokes. DON'T LET THE OIL SMOKE!)

Serve the filets with rice and garnish them with Salsa Brava, see recipe under Salad/Vegetarian, pg. 12 (Salsa Brava). Serves 4.

1996 Sunset Drive, Pacific Grove, California
Reservations: 375-7107

■ ■ ■

Critic's Choice Recipe Collection

FRESH CREAM

Marinade For Fish

5   cloves garlic, finely diced
3   oranges (juice)
1   lemon (juice)
1   Tblsp. minced basil
1   Tblsp. minced cilantro
¼   cup lite soy sauce
¼   cup salad oil
2   Tblsp. tomato puree

■

In bowl combine all ingredients, mix and pour over fish. Marinate for 1½ hours. Can be used on any type of fish, but best used with a firm, dense fish; for example, Swordfish, Ahi Tuna, or Shark. Serve with butter sauce or Hollandaise.

100 F Heritage Harbor, Monterey, California 93940
Reservations: 375-9798

■   ■   ■

Critic's Choice Recipe Collection

GERNOT'S VICTORIA HOUSE

Broiled White Fish with Saffron Sauce
on a Bed of Shiitake Mushrooms

6 oz. center cut white fish filet
2 medium Shiitake mushrooms
2 oz. butter
1 Tblsp. diced shallots
¼ cup sliced white mushrooms
¼ cup white wine
¼ cup heavy cream
1 tsp. saffron threads

■

Season fish and turn on broiler to 350°. Place under broiler for 7 minutes.

Sauce: Melt 2 oz. butter in saucepan. Add white mushrooms and half the shallots. When transparent add the white wine and saffron. Reduce by one third and add the heavy cream. Pass in a blender. Adjust seasoning and pass through a china cap. Saute Shiitake mushrooms in butter and shallots. Place white fish on top of mushrooms and carefully pour sauce around the fish. Serves 1.

649 Lighthouse Avenue, Pacific Grove, California
Reservations: 646-1477

■ ■ ■

Critic's Choice Recipe Collection

GREAT WALL

Kung Pao Seafood

½ cup medium sized shrimp, shelled and uncooked
½ cup medium sized scallops
½ cup squid filets
¼ cup carrots, sliced approx. 1 inch
¼ cup celery, sliced approx. 1 inch
¼ cup canned bamboo shoots, sliced
¼ cup green bell pepper, chopped
¼ cup white onions, chopped

Sauce:
½ cup chicken broth
1½ tsp. soy sauce
½ tsp. garlic, minced
2 dried red pepper pieces
½ tsp. sugar
1 tsp. cornstarch
½ tsp. sesame oil
⅛ tsp. white pepper
1 tsp. white wine
1 tsp. corn oil

■

Place vegetables and seafood into boiling water and cook for one minute. Do not overcook. Take out and drain.

Sauce: Brown garlic in corn oil. Add chicken broth, soy sauce, peppers, white pepper and sugar. Stir all together. Blend one teaspoon of cornstarch with two teaspoons water and mix together so there are no lumps. When sauce boils, add cornstarch mixture into sauce to thicken it.
Put cooked vegetables and seafood into sauce and stir one to two minutes more. Add sesame oil to sauce and stir. Serve over steamed rice. Serves 1.

長 城

GREAT WALL
CHINESE RESTAURANT

731 A Munras Ave., Monterey, California
Reservations: 372-3637

■ ■ ■

Critic's Choice Recipe Collection

HIGHLANDS INN

Tuna Au Poivre
with Salad Nicoise

1 lb. fresh tuna fillet, ¾" thick
1½ Tblsp. freshly cracked black pepper
2 Tblsp. olive oil
1 medium red pepper, cut into ¾" dice
1 medium red onion, cut into ¾" dice
½ lb. baby green beans,
    blanched and quickly chilled
8 small cherry tomatoes, quartered

¼ medium onion, cut into ¾" dice
8 yellow pear tomatoes, quartered
1 small head radicchio, torn
4 baby red potatoes, precooked,
    quartered
⅓ cup Italian parsley, finely chopped
12 calamata olives, pitted and slivered
¾ cup light vinaigrette dressing

■

Coat tuna liberally with pepper and refrigerate several hours or overnight. Season tuna with salt. Heat the olive oil in a skillet and sear tuna 2 minutes on each side (should be cooked rare). Remove from skillet and set aside.

To assemble the salad: Toss the vegetables, parsley and olives with vinaigrette to coat well, reserving some dressing for the tuna. Mound the vegetables on four plates with the string beans "shooting out" to enhance the presentation. Slice the tuna into ⅜" thick slices. The cross section of each slice should be dark and peppery on the outside while pink in the middle. Arrange tuna next to vegetables and drizzle with remaining vinaigrette. Serve at room temperature. Serves 4.

HIGHLANDS INN

Four Miles South of Carmel on Highway One, Carmel, California
Reservations: 624-3801

■ ■ ■

Critic's Choice Recipe Collection

KIEWEL'S

Blackened Swordfish
with Cucumber Salsa

4 7 oz. swordfish steaks
¼ tsp. black pepper
¼ tsp. white pepper
¼ tsp. granulated sugar
¼ tsp. granulated garlic
¼ tsp. salt
¼ tsp. paprika
¼ tsp. cumin
¼ tsp. oregano
½ cup oil

Cucumber Salsa:
1 cup cucumber, chopped, skinless, seedless
1 Tblsp. fresh dill
2 Tblsp. red bell pepper, chopped
½ cup vinaigrette dressing

■

Dredge swordfish in seasoning mix (pepper, sugar, garlic, salt, paprika, cumin, and oregano). Heat cast iron pan with oil until extremely hot. Sear both sides of fish until blackened (about 3 minutes per side, depending on thickness of steaks). Mix cucumber salsa ingredients together and chill. Serve over hot fish. Serves 4.

100 A Heritage Harbor, Monterey, California
Reservations: 372-6950

■ ■ ■

Critic's Choice Recipe Collection

LA BRASSERIE "Q" POINT

Grilled Salmon with Curry Olive Oil

6 oz. Atlantic salmon with skin
3 leaves fresh thyme
3 tomatoes conconsse
6 oz. extra virgin olive oil
2 Tblsp. sherry wine vinegar
1 juice from lemon
1 pinch salt
1 pinch pepper
1 Tblsp. cooked bread crumbs
   pinch curry powder
   pinch fresh garlic puree
   pinch fresh parsely, chopped

■

Put thyme on salmon. Grill salmon (with skin) over oak wood.
Put curry powder, salt, pepper, and lemon juice into a bowl and mix well. Add extra virgin olive oil and mix well again. Add sherry vinegar and mix well again. Strain the liquid.
Mix cooked bread crumbs, thyme, garlic puree and parsley. After grilling salmon, top salmon with the bread crumb mixture. Put salmon under broiler until brown. Remove from broiler and add sauce. Serves 1.

Ocean between Dolores & Lincoln, Carmel, California
Reservations: 624-2569

■ ■ ■

Critic's Choice Recipe Collection

LOS LAURELES RESTAURANT

Sea Scallops in Chardonnay-Dijon Sauce
with Red Onion Rings

2 lbs. jumbo sea scallops
1 cup chardonnay
2 Tblsp. finely chopped shallots
3 Tblsp. dijon mustard
8 oz. mushrooms, quartered
2 sprigs fresh tarragon, chopped
2 cups heavy cream
   salt and white pepper
1 medium red onion, sliced in rings
   approx. ¼ inch and grilled

■

In saute pan place chardonnay, shallots, dijon mustard, mushrooms and tarragon. Reduce on medium heat by half. Next add cream to above reduction and reduce by half. Add scallops to sauce and poach approximately 5 minutes. Scallops should remain soft. Do not allow scallops to become rubbery. Season sauce with salt and pepper. Use red onion rings placed on top for garnish.

LOS LAURELES

313 West Carmel Valley Road, Carmel Valley, California
Reservations: 659-2233

■ ■ ■

Critic's Choice Recipe Collection

MONTEREY JOE'S

Halibut with Sicilian Green Olives Provencal

2 lbs. halibut
4 tomatoes, julienne
12 Sicilian green olives
2 Tblsp. basil
4 cloves garlic
4 oz. white wine
4 oz. olive oil
    pinch crushed red pepper

■

Heat oil in saute pan, sear fish and add tomato julienne, minced basil, garlic and olives, wine and red pepper. Season with salt and pepper. Finish cooking in 500° oven. Serve fish over tomatoes. Serves 4.

2149 North Fremont, Monterey, California
Reservations: 655-3355

■   ■   ■

Critic's Choice Recipe Collection

OLD BATH HOUSE

Dungeness Crab

3 whole live Dungeness crabs
12 oz. baby spinach
1 lb. homemade linguini
1 bunch chives, chopped

Champagne Sauce:
8 oz. champagne
1½ pints heavy cream
¼ lb. butter, unsalted, cubed
1 lemon, juice
kosher salt
cayenne pepper

■

In boiling water cook crab 18 minutes. Let cool. Take meat out of the body and crack claws. Try not to damage claw meat. Cook linguini and make a ring in center of plate. Saute spinach and place in middle of pasta. Saute crab in a little butter and champagne. Place body meat on top of spinach and arrange claw meat over body meat. Top with chives and champagne sauce.

Champagne Sauce: Reduce champagne and lemon juice until ¼ inch is left in pan. Add cream. Reduce until cream coats a spoon, about $1/3$ reduction. Take off heat, add butter and whip. Season with salt and a dash of cayenne pepper. Serves 4.

Old Bath House
R E S T A U R A N T

620 Oceanview Blvd., Pacific Grove, California
Reservations: 375-5195

■　■　■

Critic's Choice Recipe Collection

PEPPERS MEXICALI CAFE

Yucatan Prawns

2 lbs. medium-large prawns shelled,
   deveined and butterflied
1 red onion, diced
2 tomatoes, diced
2 chiles, diced
1 red bell pepper, diced
¼ cup chopped cilantro
   juice of 2 oranges
   juice of 3 limes
¼ cup white wine
¼ cup fish stock
1 tsp. oregano
½ tsp. salt

■

Combine all ingredients except the prawns in a large saucepan. Cook over medium heat for 10 minutes. Add the prawns and cook for 5 minutes.
Arrange prawns in individual bowls with portions of vegetables and broth. Garnish with chopped cilantro. Offer with Salsa Cruda or Avocado Salsa. Serves 4.

170 Forest Avenue, Pacific Grove
Reservations: 373-6892

■　■　■

Critic's Choice Recipe Collection

RIO GRILL

Grilled Swordfish
with Avocado Papaya Sauce

6 6 oz. swordfish steaks

Grilling Mixture
½ cup mild olive oil
1 Tblsp. garlic, chopped
   salt and pepper to taste

Avocado Papaya Salsa:
4 ripe papayas peeled, seeded, and
   medium diced
4 Haas avocados peeled, seeded
   and medium diced
3 tsp. red onion, finely diced
⅛ tsp. red chili flakes
3 Tblsp. fresh lime juice
3 Tblsp. sour cream

■

Preheat BBQ grill. Lightly brush swordfish with olive oil mixture and sprinkle with salt and pepper to taste. Grill until medium rare, turning once about 4 minutes per side. Divide salsa among 6 warm dinner plates and serve swordfish on top of sauce. Crisscross 2 long chives over the top.

Salsa: Gently combine all ingredients. Use within 2 hours since salsa will begin to break up after that. Serves 6.

Highway One & Rio Road, Carmel, California
Reservations: 625-5436

■ ■ ■

Critic's Choice Recipe Collection

SANDBAR & GRILL

Paperwrapped Halibut with Lime Butter
and Sauteed Mushrooms

4 8 oz. halibut filets
½ lb. butter
   zest of lime
   chopped green onion
   sliced mushrooms

■

Preheat oven to 350°. Saute onions, mushrooms, and lime in butter. Put each halibut filet on bakers paper. Evenly distribute sauteed mixture over fish. Wrap and bake for 20 minutes. Serve with julienne zuchinni and carrots. Serves 4.

Wharf #2, Monterey, California
Information: 373-2818

■ ■ ■

Critic's Choice Recipe Collection

SANS SOUCI

Crevettes au Curry Avec Sauce Composée
Prawns with Curry, Coconut Milk & Cucumbers

1½ lbs. peeled & deveined prawns
1   8 oz. can coconut milk
1   Tblsp. curry powder
1   clove garlic, minced
1   cucumber, peeled & diced
1   Tblsp. olive oil

■

Saute prawns in olive oil. Add minced garlic, curry powder, cucumbers and coconut milk. Cook until prawns become bright red and sauce is thick. Serves 4.

Sans Souci

French Cuisine

Lincoln between 5th & 6th Ave., Carmel, California
Reservations: 624-6220

■   ■   ■

Critic's Choice Recipe Collection

SPADARO'S RISTORANTE

Pasta Carciofa (Artichokes)

8 oz. fresh fettuccine
1 oz. fresh basil
  pinch saffron
6 to 8 artichoke hearts, chopped
1 quart heavy cream
4 to 8 large prawns
1 oz. proscuitto, chopped

■

Saute proscuitto until cooked. Add prawns and saute for 5 minutes. Add artichoke hearts, stir in heavy cream. Reduce until it thickens. Add pinch of saffron.
Cook fettuccine in boiling water for 5-8 minutes, then toss into sauce and serve.
Serves 2.

Spadaro's
RISTORANTE

650 Cannery Row, Monterey, California
Reservations: 372-8881

■   ■   ■

Critic's Choice Recipe Collection

TASTE CAFE & BISTRO

Ahi Tuna
with Fresh Italian Tomato Salsa

7 oz. Ahi tuna
6 or 8 medium red vine ripened tomatoes
   peeled, seeded and diced
½ bunch Italian parsley, chopped
1 small red onion, diced
4 Tblsp. champagne vinegar
2 Tblsp. extra virgin olive oil
4 Tblsp. fresh basil, chopped
   juice of 3 to 4 lemons
1 tsp. fresh garlic, chopped
   salt and pepper

■

Combine all ingredients and adjust seasonings. Salt and pepper tuna. Sear in a hot
saute pan with small amount of olive oil for 1–2 minutes. Cook rare to medium rare
or grill on a gas grill 2–3 minutes. Place tuna on plates and spoon salsa on top.
Garnish with 3 Kalamata olives and serve with fresh cooked green beans.
Serves 4–6.

TaSte
CAFE & BISTRO

1199 Forest Avenue, Pacific Grove, California
Reservations: 655-0324

■   ■   ■

Critic's Choice Recipe Collection

THE FABULOUS TOOT'S LAGOON

Caribbean "Jerk" Style Calamari Strips

2   5-6 oz. jumbo calamari steaks
2   oz. sliced bell pepper
2   oz. canned pineapple chunks
2   oz. sliced mushrooms
2   oz. cooking oil (peanut oil will be best)
1   Tblsp. "Jerk" spice
    or Island Spice seasoning

■

Cut calamari steak into strips that are approximately 1 oz. in weight. In a pot of boiling water blanch calamari strips for thirty seconds. Remove from water and drain excess water. In a medium hot saute pan add oil and heat. Next add peppers, mushrooms, pineapple chunks, and spice. Quickly saute vegetables for about 30 seconds. Now add blanched calamari strips to pan and cook for about one minute. Serves 2.

Dolores Between Ocean & 7th, Pacific Grove, California
Reservations: 625-1915

■   ■   ■

Critic's Choice Recipe Collection

THE TINNERY

Red Snapper
with Red Wine Sauce

 4   6 oz. red snapper filets
12   oz. shallots
 1   Tblsp. butter
 2   cloves garlic
½   cup red wine vinegar
 2   cups chicken stock
⅓   lb. butter, softened
     salt and pepper

■

Saute fish in hot oil until done. Serve with sauce.

Sauce: Saute shallots in butter until tender. Add garlic, vinegar and wine. Reduce to around 2 cups. Before serving, warm stock, not hot, and beat in softened butter. Serves 4.

tinnery
AT THE BEACH

631 Oceanview Blvd., Pacific Grove, California
Reservations: 646-1040

■ ■ ■

Critic's Choice Recipe Collection

POULTRY

ANTON & MICHEL

Chicken Jerusalem

4 full breasts of chicken (with skin on)
10 oz. artichoke hearts, halved
8 oz. mushrooms, quartered
¼ cup olive oil
½ tsp. thyme (dried & crushed)
½ tsp. oregano (dried & crushed)
1 Tblsp. shallots
1 Tblsp. garlic
½ cup dry white wine
1 cup heavy cream
   salt & ground pepper

■

Place the artichoke hearts in a pot of cold water, add ½ tsp. salt, bring the water to boil then simmer for approximately 10 minutes. Drain and keep aside.
Salt & pepper the chicken breasts. Heat the olive oil in a skillet, saute the chicken until all sides are nice and brown (about 10 minutes on medium heat). Remove chicken from skillet and place in a warm spot. Add garlic, shallots and mushrooms to the skillet, saute until mushrooms are half cooked. Deglaze pan with dry white wine and add the thyme and oregano. Reduce by half then add the artichoke hearts, cream and chicken. Cook for about 10 minutes on high heat and reduce until sauce is thick.
Taste and season accordingly. Serves 4.

Anton
&
Michel

Mission Between Ocean & Seventh, Carmel, California
Reservations: 624-2406

■ ■ ■

Critic's Choice Recipe Collection

BEAU THAI

Kai P'ad King
Chicken Ginger

1 Tblsp. vegetable oil
½ tsp. garlic, chopped
½ cup chicken, cut in small
   bite-sized pieces
⅓ cup ginger, peeled & cut in small strips
⅓ cup Japanese black mushrooms, ¼" slices
1 Tblsp. oyster sauce
½ cup green onions, cut in 1" pieces
1 cup cabbage, chopped

■

Stir fry first 3 ingredients until chicken is tender. Add rest of ingredients. Stir fry for a minute and a half and serve. Serves 2.

DAVID WALTON'S
BEAU THAI
RESTAURANT

807 Cannery Row, Monterey, California
Reservations: 373-8811

Critic's Choice Recipe Collection

BINDEL'S

Grilled Smoked Chicken Breast

4 8 oz. chicken breasts, ½ smoked
4 oz. Shitake mushrooms
4 oz. Oyster mushrooms
4 oz. Crimini mushrooms
1 oz. brandy
   Kosher salt
1 oz. butter, unsalted

Rosemary Garlic Butter:
6 oz. Chardonnay
6 cloves garlic, chopped
1 half-pint heavy cream
   Kosher salt
   fresh rosemary

■

Lightly smoke chicken, grill skin side down first to get a nice crisp skin. In a saute pan, heat 1 oz. butter, add mushrooms. When half cooked, add brandy and a few pinches of salt.

Rosemary Garlic Butter:
Reduce Chardonnay and garlic until only ¼" is left in sauce pan. Add cream, reduce until cream coats a spoon. Take off heat, add cubed butter, whip until totally incorporated, season, add fresh rosemary. Serves 4.

Bindel's

500 Hartnell, Monterey, California
Reservations: 373-3737

■   ■   ■

Critic's Choice Recipe Collection

CENTRAL 159

Thyme and Roasted Garlic Hen

8 1 lb. whole game hens
4 whole lemons
16 Tblsp. balsamic vinegar
16 sprigs fresh thyme or rosemary
4 heads roasted garlic,
    picked and pasted with 3 Tblsp. olive oil
    salt and black pepper

Roasted Garlic:
6 whole heads garlic,
    jumbo or extra large
1½ cups good olive oil
    salt and white pepper

■

Preheat oven to 400°. Lightly rinse game hens and pat dry. Season each cavity liberally with salt and black pepper. Break one stem of herb of choice in half and place in each cavity. Remaining herbs should be picked, chopped, and set aside. Half each lemon and place 1 half into the cavity of each hen. Fold wings under and tie the legs together with twine. Place hens on a foil covered baking sheet. Coat each hen evenly with the roasted garlic paste. Drizzle each hen with 2 Tblsp. balsamic vinegar. Sprinkle remaining herbs over hens, season with salt and black pepper. Bake approximately 45 minutes until golden brown.
To serve: remove string ties and empty the cavity. Dress and serve. Serves 8.

Roasted Garlic: Cut off tops of garlic about ⅛ inch down from the top. Place in shallow baking pan and cover with the oil. Some of the oil should sit in the bottom of the pan. Season with salt and pepper. Cover with foil and bake at 400° for approximately 45 to 60 minutes. The garlic should begin to pop up and will be tender to the touch.

159 Central Avenue, Pacific Grove, California
Reservations: 372-2235

■   ■   ■

Critic's Choice Recipe Collection

CLUB XIX

Barbecue Breast of Chicken
with Fire Roasted Red Onions and Grilled Red Potatoes

6   8 oz. chicken breasts - wing bone attached
2   large red onions
12   red potatoes
⅓ cup red wine vinegar
2   Tblsp. sugar
¼ cup olive oil
½ bunch thyme finely minced
    salt and pepper to taste

■

Cut potatoes in half and coat with olive oil and minced thyme. Salt and pepper
lightly. Roast potatoes in 400° oven for 15 minutes. Remove potatoes from oven and
let cool to room temperature. Skewer potatoes with small wooden skewers, also
reserve olive oil and thyme marinade.
Peel red onion and cut width wise into 3 sections. Place each section onto
individually cut foil and drizzle equal amounts of sugar and red wine vinegar over
each red onion section. Wrap foil tightly around red onion. Reserve.
Once coals on barbecue begin to turn grey, bury foil wrapped red onions in coals.
Brush chicken breasts with reserved olive oil marinade and grill, skin side down.
Turn chicken often. Chicken breasts should grill approximately 8 - 10 minutes.
When chicken breasts are half cooked, place skewered potatoes on grill, turning
often. Remove chicken breasts, potatoes and red onions from barbecue and serve.
Serves 6.

C   L   U   B

The Lodge at Pebble Beach, 17 Mile Drive
Reservations: 624-3811

■   ■   ■

Critic's Choice Recipe Collection

CYPRESS ROOM

Seared Chicken Breast
with Shitake Mushrooms, Ginger and Scallion Sauce

 2 ea. 8 oz. chicken breasts
    flour to dredge chicken
 2 oz. clarified butter
 2 cloves garlic, crushed
 1 Tblsp. diced ginger
 2 oz. oyster sauce
 1 oz. sesame oil
 1 oz. water
 8″ and 6″ saute pans

■

Heat 8″ pan and add 1 oz. butter. Dredge chicken in flour and sear in hot butter until browned on both sides. Put in 375° oven to finish cooking. In 6″ pan add remaining butter and saute Shitake mushrooms and garlic. Remove from pan and hold. Take chicken out of oven and from pan. Add rest of ingredients and let simmer to make a sauce. Serve the chicken on top of the cooked mushrooms. Ladle sauce over the chicken. Serves 2.

THE CYPRESS ROOM

The Lodge at Pebble Beach, 17 Mile Drive
Reservations: 624-3811

■ ■ ■

Critic's Choice Recipe Collection

DELFINO'S ON THE BAY

Chicken Breast with Artichokes & Roasted Bell Peppers

4   whole boneless chicken breasts
2   large artichokes
1   yellow bell pepper
1   red bell pepper
1   cup Gewvertztraminer (or dry white wine)
6   oz. butter
2   oz. all purpose flour
1   oz. granulated garlic
1   oz. minced garlic
2   oz. olive oil
4   bay leaves
    salt and black pepper

■

Cook the artichokes whole in ½ gallon boiling water, seasoned with 1 oz. salt and ½ oz. granulated garlic and 4 bay leaves. Simmer for about 10 - 15 minutes or until artichokes are tender. Drain half of the water and replace with ice. This will "shock" the artichokes and keep them from getting too soft. Set aside.
Remove skin from chicken breasts and trim all fat. Place in fridge.
Roast the bell peppers. This can be done in either the oven, preheated to the max (broiler) or on an outdoor BBQ. Both methods require turning of the bell peppers until they are black all around and the skin can be easily removed. Cut the bell peppers in julienne and set aside.
In the meantime the artichokes should be cooled enough. Trim all outer leaves and remove the "hair" on the inside. Cut the artichokes in small pieces.
In a skillet heat the oil. Season the chicken breasts with salt and pepper and dip them in flour. Brown them over medium heat on each side for approximately 2 minutes. Add garlic, bell peppers, artichokes and wine. Let simmer for about 7 minutes over medium heat. When the chicken is almost done increase the heat and let wine reduce by half. Cut the butter in small chunks and add to the sauce. Turn heat off and stir until all the butter is worked into the sauce. Do not boil the sauce or it might seperate. Place chicken breast on platter and pour the sauce over it. Garnish with Italian parsley. Serve with roasted potatoes or rice.
Serves 4.

Delfino's
ON THE BAY

Monterey Plaza Hotel, 400 Cannery Row, Monterey, California
Reservations: 646-1706

■   ■   ■

Critic's Choice Recipe Collection

DIÁNA

Chicken Galileo

4 oz. boneless & skinless chicken breasts
12 medium mushrooms, quartered
20 small prawns
1 Tblsp. fresh herbs, chopped
(thyme, oregano, basil & rosemary)
1 cup white wine
¼ lb. butter, sweetcream
3 Tblsp. all purpose flour
1 pint heavy cream
salt and pepper to taste

■

Preheat oven to 400°. Saute chicken in ⅛ lb. sweet butter. Sprinkle both sides
generously with herbs and salt and pepper to taste. Add shrimp and finsh in the
oven at 400°.
When cooked, remove from pan and add remaining butter and melt. Add flour until
consistent. Deglaze with white wine and simmer for 30 seconds. Add cream, salt
and pepper. Pour sauce over chicken. Serve with rice and vegetables. Serves 4.

Carmel Plaza, Ocean & Junipero, Carmel, California
Reservations: 626-0191

■ ■ ■

Critic's Choice Recipe Collection

EL COCODRILO

Jamaican Style BBQ Chicken
with Pineapple Salsa

4   chicken breasts, leave skin on
2   Tblsp. oil
2   Tblsp. *Jamaican Jerk seasoning

Pineapple Salsa:
1   cup diced fresh pineapple
½   cup diced jicama
½   cup diced tomato
1   Tblsp. chopped fresh dill
1   serrano chili, minced
¼   cup diced red bell pepper

■

Rub chicken breasts with oil. Then sprinkle the jerk spices over the chicken. Rub the mixture lightly into the meat and skin and then let it "penetrate" for 4 hours. Barbecue or grill the breasts. Remove the skin if you wish. Serve the breasts garnished with the Pineapple Salsa.

Pineapple Salsa: Mix the above ingredients together; use the salsa as a garnish for the Jamaican Style BBQ Chicken. Serves 4.

* Jerk is available in some supermarkets and at El Cocodrilo

El Cocodrilo

ROTISSERIE and SEAFOOD GRILL

701 Lighthouse Avenue, Pacific Grove, California
Reservations: 655-3311

■   ■   ■

Critic's Choice Recipe Collection

FANDANGO

Poulet Basquaise

3 lb. chicken, cut into pieces
   flour
3 Tblsp. olive oil
2 cloves garlic
½ lb. fresh mushrooms, quartered
5 medium sized tomatoes, diced
5 oz. ham, diced
1 green bell pepper, sliced
1 red bell pepper, sliced
¾ cup dry white wine
   salt and pepper to taste
   pinch of cumin
   raspberry vinegar

■

Toss chicken pieces in flour. In heavy cast iron casserole rubbed with garlic cloves
add chicken and brown over medium heat.
Add quartered mushrooms and quickly saute with browned chicken. Stir in
tomatoes. Add ham and bell peppers.
Add wine, salt, pepper, cumin and touch of vinegar. Cover with heavy lid and
simmer until done (about 20–30 minutes).
Remove chicken pieces when cooked and reduce sauce over high heat until desired
thickness of sauce is achieved. Pour over chicken and serve. Serves 4.

fandango

223 17th St., Pacific Grove, California
Reservations: 372-3456

■   ■   ■

Critic's Choice Recipe Collection

FIFI'S CAFE & BAKERY

Rosemary and Garlic Chicken Breasts

6 boneless chicken breasts
4 Tblsp. olive oil
4 Tblsp. finely chopped fresh rosemary
   pepper to taste
2 Tblsp. olive oil
½ cup dry white wine
3 Tblsp. garlic, chopped
3 Tblsp. shallots, chopped

■

Marinate the chicken breast with 4 Tblsp. olive oil, ¼ cup white wine, and fresh rosemary overnight, if possible. In a frying pan put the 2 Tblsp. olive oil and saute the chicken for 2 to 3 minutes on the first side. Turn over and cook until the meat is golden. Add the remaining wine, the garlic, and shallots and cook for an additional minute. Add salt and pepper to taste. Serve immediately with rice and fresh vegetables. Serves 6.

Fifi's Cafe
& BAKERY

1188 Forest Avenue, Pacific Grove, California
Reservations: 372-5235

■ ■ ■

Critic's Choice Recipe Collection

FISHWIFE AT ASILOMAR BEACH

Chicken Breast Criollo

4   boneless chicken breasts,
    pounded to ¼ inch thick

Marinade:
4   oz. soy sauce
4   oz. peanut oil
1   tsp. Cajun spices
1   tsp. black pepper
1   Tblsp. achiote paste
1   tsp. pureed garlic

■

Mix the marinade ingredients together and coat each chicken breast. Allow the chicken to marinate for two hours before cooking. Grill the breasts or saute them for three minutes on each side. Serve garnished with pickled Bermuda onions. Serves 4.

1996 Sunset Drive, Pacific Grove, California
Reservations: 375-7017

■   ■   ■

Critic's Choice Recipe Collection

FRESH CREAM

Turkey, Pheasant, and Chicken Breast Sausage
Wrapped in Puff Pastry

    1   turkey breast, skin removed
    1   pheasant breast, skin removed
    1   chicken breast, skin removed
    8   oz. pork back fat
    1   cup milk
    2   bay leaves
    1   sprig thyme
        salt & pepper
    2   Tblsp. garlic, finely diced
    2   Tblsp. shallots, finely diced
        Puff Pastry
        egg

■

Grind turkey, pheasant, chicken breasts and fat. Saute garlic and shallots and add to mixture. Scald milk with bay leaves, thyme, salt and pepper. Incorporate scalded milk into mixture. Mix very well. Test a little in a pan to check for seasoning. Wrap in puff pastry using egg wash to seal. Bake at 325° for 30 minutes. Let cool. Slice. Reheat until pastries puff up and serve. Serves 6–8.

100 F Heritage Harbor, Monterey, California
Reservations: 375-9798

■   ■   ■

Critic's Choice Recipe Collection

GERNOT'S VICTORIA HOUSE

Broiled Herb Chicken

2½ lbs. chicken, quartered
 6 Tblsp. butter
    parsley sprigs
1½ tsp. dried thyme
    salt and pepper
1–2 Tblsp. vegetable oil

■

Lift the skin of the chicken quarters carefully with your finger, being careful not to tear the skin or detach it except from the main part of the flesh. In so doing there will be pockets. Soften the butter. Chop several large parsley sprigs and blend them into the butter until you have a slightly greenish paste. Add the thyme.
Smear the paste all over the flesh of the chicken under the skin until you have a good thick coating. Fold back the skin into its normal position and press down firmly. Sprinkle the chicken with salt and pepper.
Place the chicken on a rack in the broiling pan, skin side down, and broil 4 inches from the heat source for 20 minutes. Baste the pieces once with oil. Turn them, baste again, and continue to broil 20 more minutes. Baste with juices and additional oil if necessary. The chicken will be crisp and brown when done. Serves 4.

649 Lighthouse Avenue, Pacific Grove, California
Reservations: 646-1477

■ ■ ■

Critic's Choice Recipe Collection

GREAT WALL

Orange Chicken

1   chicken breast, lean, skinned & boned
3   Tblsp. water chestnut powder
1   tsp. white vinegar
1½ tsp. soy sauce
5   tsp. sugar
½   tsp. sesame oil
½   tsp. garlic, minced
½   tsp. cornstarch
½   cup chicken broth
4   pieces dried orange peel *
1   ½" round slice of fresh orange
     cut into 4 pieces
1   dried red chili pepper broken in half

■

Cut chicken breasts into 8 pieces. Coat with water chestnut powder and deep fry in corn oil for ten minutes or until golden brown and crispy.
In wok, place vinegar, soy sauce, sugar, sesame oil, garlic, chicken broth, orange pieces, and red chili pepper. Melt sugar and blend all ingredients.
Mix cornstarch with 1 tsp. water and blend to eliminate lumps. Stir corn starch mixture into sauce to thicken. Add cooked chicken and toss in sauce (don't leave in sauce too long). Take out orange peel. Place chicken on a bed of steamed rice and serve. Serves 1.

* can be purchased in Chinese Market.

長 城

GREAT WALL
CHINESE RESTAURANT

731 A Munras Avenue, Monterey, California
Reservations: 372-3637

■   ■   ■

Critic's Choice Recipe Collection

HIGHLANDS INN

Roast Chicken with Sweet Garlic

4 2½-3 pound chickens (fryers)	2 large onions
15 large spinach leaves, washed	2 ribs celery
4 oz. fresh Foie Gras (domestic)	1 large carrot
2 Tblsp. butter	4 bulbs garlic
40 cloves of fresh garlic	2 bay leaves
Sauce:	2 litres water
1 litre red wine	1 bunch marjoram

■

Procedure: Remove breasts from both sides of chicken so as to yield 2 half-breasts with wing attached. Remove both thigh portions and take out the thigh bone. With a mallet, pound the thighs so that they are ¼ inch thick. Melt butter in skillet. Add spinach and cook just until wilted. Season with salt and pepper and place on towel to absorb moisture. Place spinach leaves on pounded chicken thighs, skin-side facing the table, just to cover meat. Slice Foie Gras into eighths and wrap in a spinach leaf. Place on middle of thigh. Tie the "Roulade" with butcher twine twice, so the meat is tight.

Sauce: Roast in a 450° oven until golden brown. Half way, add 2 onions and 4 garlic bulbs, sliced in half with skin on, and brown with the bones. Deglaze pan with red wine, transfer to stove top, and reduce by two thirds. Add water, carrot and celery, sliced in one-inch pieces, bay leaves, and marjoram, and simmer until reduced by half. Strain through fine sieve, and reserve.

Garnish: Remove whole garlic cloves from husk, place in aluminum foil, drizzle with olive oil and bake for 45 minutes until soft and golden.

To Serve: Season chicken breasts and thighs with salt and pepper. In a skillet, place one tablespoon of olive oil, chicken and sauce, (skin side down on the breast), until golden on both sides. Place in 400° oven for five minutes for the breasts and 10 minutes for the thighs. Remove from oven and let rest. Cut string off thighs. Drizzle 1 oz. of sauce over meat. Place five garlic cloves around plate. Serves 8.

HIGHLANDS INN

Four Miles South of Carmel on Highway One, Carmel, California
Reservations: 624-3801

■　■　■

Critic's Choice Recipe Collection

KIEWEL'S

Grilled Breast of Chicken
with Raspberry Sauce

4 8 oz. chicken breasts - boneless, skinless
½ cup raspberry vinegar
1 Tblsp. sugar
1 Tblsp. raspberry preserves
¼ tsp. fresh chopped garlic
1 cup demi-glace (reduced veal stock)
1 pint fresh raspberry

■

In medium stock pan, reduce the vinegar, sugar, preserves and garlic to half of original volume. Add the demi-glace and simmer for 10 to 15 minutes.
Grill or BBQ chicken breasts. Add fresh raspberry to sauce and serve over chicken breast. Serves 4.

100 A Heritage Harbor, Monterey, California
Reservations: 372-6950

■ ■ ■

Critic's Choice Recipe Collection

LA BRASSERIE "Q" POINT

Rolled Chicken Breast
Stuffed with Wild Mushroom Mousse and Tarragon Cream

6 chicken breasts, 8 oz. pieces
1 lb. coul fat
2 oz. chicken mousse

Chicken Mousse Stuffing:
1 chicken breast
1 egg
¼ quart cream
1 pinch pepper
1 tsp. minced garlic
1 tsp. parsely

½ lb. shitake mushrooms
½ lb. oyster mushrooms
1 Tblsp. butter
3 oz. shallots

Tarragon Cream Sauce:
1 lb. beef stock
¾ quart cream
1 Tblsp. butter
1 fresh chopped tarragon

■

Remove skin and bones from 1 chicken breast. Cut chicken into small pieces and puree in food processor with 1 egg. Add pinch of salt and pepper and ¼ quart of cream.

Put butter and garlic in saucepan with chopped shallots. Add chopped oyster and shitake mushrooms to saucepan and cook until lightly browned. Cool. Mix chicken mousse and mushrooms in a bowl. Add 1 Tblsp. parsley to complete the chicken mousse.

Wrap coul fat around each chicken breast. Saute chicken breast in oil and butter until lightly browned and place in oven at 380° for 17 minutes.

Sauce: Add 1 lb. beef stock to sauce pan and reduce to 4 oz. over medium heat. Add cream, tarragon, salt, pepper and butter. Cook over medium heat.

Cut each chicken breast into 5 pieces and pour tarragon cream sauce over and serve. Serves 4.

La Brasserie
QPoint
of Carmel

Ocean between Dolores & Lincoln, Carmel, California
Reservations: 624-2569

■ ■ ■

Critic's Choice Recipe Collection

LOS LAURELES RESTAURANT

Roasted Quail
Filled with Veal Mousse and Panchetta

2 quail per person, completely boned
1 lb. lean veal - cubed
   ice
2 eggs
½ cup cream
½ tsp. ground sage
½ oz. brandy
   salt, white pepper
¼ lb. Panchetta - diced
¼ lb. sliced mushrooms
½ cup dry Marsala

■

Mousse: In food processor puree - veal, a little ice and salt & pepper. Add sage and brandy. Gradually add eggs and lastly cream. Remove from processor bowl and fold in diced Panchetta.

Stuff each quail and close with a toothpick. Brown quail in saute pan with a little olive oil and bake in 425° oven for 15–20 minutes. Remove quail from pan, add mushrooms and marsala. Reduce by ½, add an ounce of butter and season to taste. Serve one quail whole and the other cut. Sauce goes directly over top. Serves 4.

LOS LAURELES

313 West Carmel Valley Road, Carmel Valley, California
Reservations: 659-2233

■　■　■

Critic's Choice Recipe Collection

MONTEREY JOE'S

Oven Roasted Chicken

2 chickens, whole
2 lemons, whole
1 onion, large
4 sprigs rosemary
4 cloves garlic
2 oz. butter
2 oz. olive oil

■

Chop lemons, onions, rosemary and garlic. Season heavily with salt and pepper. Stuff into chicken and tie opening with string. Coat outside of chicken with butter and olive oil, season heavily. Roast in oven at 450° for ten minutes then turn down to 325° for approx. 25 minutes or until juices run clear. Make sauce from stuffing and drippings. Do not eat stuffing. Serves 4.

2149 North Fremont, Monterey, California
Reservations: 655-3355

■　　■　　■

Critic's Choice Recipe Collection

OLD BATH HOUSE

Duck Merlot

3-5 lb. Mapleleaf duck
  6 bay leaves
  1 bunch thyme
      Kosher salt

Merlot Sauce:
  ¼ cup sugar
  2 oz. Raspberry vinegar
  3 cups Merlot wine
  3 cups demi-glace - brown stock

■

Preparation time 2 days.
Cut meat off bones keeping it intact, save all fat. Separate breasts from legs, trim around meat so there is only ⅛ of an inch of fat as a border.
In a pan approximately 3 inches deep, place a thin layer of salt, crumbled up bay leaves and chopped thyme. Lay duck on top and put the same ingredients on top of duck. Marinate 24 hours.
Cut up all fat into 1 inch pieces. Fat should be saved from all trim and any pieces left on the bone. Place in pot with 1½ cups water, boil down until clear and all the water has evaporated. Strain.
Brown duck on skin side first, turn and brown meat side, cover with remaining rendered fat and cook at a low simmer for 1 hour. Remove and let fat and meat cool. Place in a container and cover with cooled off fat. If fat covers duck no air will penetrate and it will store up to 2 months in refrigerator.
For best results, make one week in advance. This will tenderize duck.
To serve place skin side down and cook at 400° for twenty minutes or until skin crisps up.

Merlot Sauce: Place sugar and vinegar in sauce pan, lightly brown. Add Merlot and reduce until ¼ inch is left in pan. Add demi-glace, reduce until it coats a spoon. Season with kosher salt. Serves 6.

Old Bath House
R E S T A U R A N T

620 Oceanview Boulevard, Pacific Grove, California
Reservations: 375-5195

■ ■ ■

Critic's Choice Recipe Collection

PEPPERS MEXICALI CAFE

Chicken Caribe
with Tropical Fruit Salsa Fresca

4   8 oz. boneless, skinless chicken breasts

Marinade:
2   oz. fresh lime juice
2   oz. fresh lemon juice
4   oz. orange juice
2   oz. peanut oil
3   cloves garlic, minced
½   small red onion, diced
½   bunch cilantro, chopped
½   tsp. habanero sauce (optional)

Tropical Salsa:
1   mango, skinned & chopped
1   papaya, skinned, seeded
     & chopped

1   small jicama,
     peeled & chopped
1   red bell pepper,
     chopped small
½   small red onion, diced
2   cloves garlic, minced
½   bunch cilantro, chopped
1   fresh jalapeno,
     seeded & diced
2   oz. lime juice
2   oz. lemon juice
3   oz. orange juice
     red pepper flakes (optional)

■

Combine all marinade ingredients and mix well.
Combine all tropical salsa ingredients and mix well.
Wash and trim all fat and skin from chicken breasts. Marinate covered and
refrigerate 2 hours or more. Grill or broil until done and top with salsa.
Serve with black beans, rice and tortillas. Serves 4.

170 Forest Avenue, Pacific Grove, California
Reservations: 373-6892

■   ■   ■

Critic's Choice Recipe Collection

RIO GRILL

Rotisserie of Duck

1   4-5 lb. duckling
½ tsp. salt
4   Tblsp. fresh thyme leaf
1   jar orange marmalade
½ cup chicken stock
2   oranges, quartered
3   cloves garlic, crushed
1   cup orange juice, fresh squeezed

■

Light the barbeque. Remove neck, liver and gizzard from duck. Rinse cavity with cold water and pat dry with paper towels. Rub cavity with salt and half the amount of thyme. Stuff cavity with crushed garlic and quartered oranges. Truss the bird. Prick the flesh to release fat. Set aside and let marinate 1-2 hours.
In a sauce pan combine orange juice, marmalade, chicken stock and remaining thyme. Bring to a boil and simmer 15 minutes. Remove from heat and set aside until ready to use.
Secure duck on rotisserie and, with the lid of barbeque closed, cook it over medium-hot coals.
After duck has cooked for 30 minutes, generously brush the skin with glaze every 5-10 minutes, until it is done.
The total cooking time is approximately 50 minutes. The duck is done when the juices run rose color for medium or clear for well done. Serves 4.

Highway One & Rio Road, Carmel, California
Reservations: 625-5436

■   ■   ■

Critic's Choice Recipe Collection

SANDBAR & GRILL

Chicken Breast Piccatta

8 5 oz. chicken breasts
2 oz. capers
12 oz. white wine
    juice from half lemon
4 oz. chicken consome
¼ lb. butter
1 tsp. arrowroot

■

Mix all ingredients, except chicken and arrowroot. Bring to simmer. Add arrowroot to thicken sauce. Pour over charbroiled or panfried breast. Serve with broccoli or asparagus as a side dish. Serves 4.

Wharf # 2, Monterey, California
Information: 373-2818

■   ■   ■

Critic's Choice Recipe Collection

SANS SOUCI

Ballotine de Volaille aux Epinards
Chicken Breast filled with Spinach, Mushroom Sauce

4 double chicken breasts, boneless
2 bunches fresh spinach
1 lb. medium mushrooms
⅛ cup cooking sherry
½ cup cream
   salt and white pepper
1 clove garlic, minced

■

Cook spinach and squeeze the excess water out. Season with salt, garlic and white pepper. Stuff the breasts equally with spinach. Roast breasts in oiled dish for 30 minutes at 400°.
Meanwhile slice mushrooms, cook them in sherry, add cream and reduce until sauce is thick. Pour over roasted chicken breasts. Serve very hot. Serves 4.

Sans Souci

French Cuisine

Lincoln between 5th & 6th Avenue, Carmel, California
Reservations: 624-6220

■   ■   ■

Critic's Choice Recipe Collection

SPADARO'S RISTORANTE

Chicken San Remo

10 oz. chicken breast, pounded
 1 Tblsp. dijon mustard
    pinch basil
 1 oz. roasted pistachio nuts, crushed
    salt & pepper to taste
    flour
 2 Tblsp. oil
¼ cup wine, preferably Sauvignon Blanc
    onion, diced
    garlic, diced

Roux:
½ lb. butter
    flour

■

Pound chicken breast. Lay flat and rub dijon mustard, basil, salt, pepper and pistachios. Roll up and flour chicken. Put into pan with hot oil and cook for 5 minutes over high flame. Keep turning chicken. Drain oil. Finish in 400° oven for 10–12 minutes.

Stock: Should be made with bones from chicken. Saute onion and garlic until browned. Add chicken bones and water (¼ bones to ¾ water). Add wine salt, pepper, and garlic. Simmer 2 hours. Drain bones & vegetables into strainer and reduce stock in half until thickened.

Roux: Melt butter and whisk in flour until it tightens.

Sauce: Add Sauvignon Blanc, basil, salt and pepper to finished stock. Add Roux to sauce until it thickens. Top over chicken breast. Serves 1.

Spadaro's RISTORANTE

650 Cannery Row, Monterey, California
Reservations: 372-8881

■ ■ ■

Critic's Choice Recipe Collection

TASTE CAFE & BISTRO

Italian Chicken with Artichokes

```
 2  6 oz. jars marinated artichoke hearts
 6  Tblsp. olive oil
¼  cup flour
16  chicken breasts, boned and skinned
 8  medium tomatoes, peeled, seeded
    and quartered
 4  garlic cloves, minced
 2  small onions, diced
1½  lbs. fresh mushrooms, sliced
 1  cup dry sherry
 1  tsp. dried oregano
 2  tsp. dried basil
    salt and fresh ground pepper to taste
```

■

Saute garlic and onions to carmelize, stirring constantly. Sear mushrooms in separate pan in hot oil and add to garlic/onion mixture. Add dry sherry, tomatoes, artichoke hearts, oregano, basil, salt and pepper. Simmer for 20 minutes.

To Prepare Chicken Breasts: Salt, pepper and flour chicken breasts, shaking off excess flour. Brown chicken breasts in hot oil over medium high heat for 3-5 minutes. Drain slightly. Transfer chicken breasts to baking pan and bake 10 minutes in 350° oven.

Arrange each plate with angel hair pasta, cooked al dente and lightly oiled. Serve two chicken breasts on top of pasta and spoon sauce on top of chicken. Garnish with freshly grated parmesan cheese and finely chopped Italian parsley. Serves 8.

TaSte
CAFE & BISTRO

1199 Forest Avenue, Pacific Grove, California
Reservations: 655-0324

■ ■ ■

Critic's Choice Recipe Collection

THE FABULOUS TOOT'S LAGOON

Sicillian Chicken

2 9-10 oz. chicken breasts, boneless
4 oz. dry Marsala
4 oz. demi-glace
2 oz. heavy cream
1 Tblsp. honey
¼ tsp. whole rosemary
1 bay leaf
1 Tblsp. butter

■

Remove skin from chicken breasts and gently pound with mallet until about ⅛ inch thick. Poach chicken in white wine (chablis or chardonnay) until cooked through. Remove from wine and set aside. In a saute pan add wine and reduce to ½ original volume. Add demi-glace, honey, rosemary and bay leaf. Gently reduce for about two minutes. Add heavy cream and butter slowly heat until sauce boils. Strain sauce and place chicken breasts and sauce into a clean saute pan. Heat slowly for one minute then serve. Serves 2.

Dolores between Ocean & 7th, Carmel, California
Reservations: 625-1915

■   ■   ■

Critic's Choice Recipe Collection

THE TINNERY

Chicken Mexicali

2   8 oz. chicken breasts
1   tomato,diced
⅓   onion, diced
1   Tblsp. chopped cilantro
½   tsp. lemon juice
    salt and pepper

■

Saute chicken breasts until done. Mix together tomato, onion, cilantro, lemon juice, salt and pepper and serve on top of chicken. Serves 2.

631 Oceanview Boulevard, Pacific Grove, California
Reservations: 646-1040

■   ■   ■

Critic's Choice Recipe Collection

MEAT

ANTON & MICHEL

Kufta Kebab

1 lb. lean ground lamb or beef
1 medium onion, finely chopped or grated
½ cup parsley, finely chopped
1 tsp. salt
1 pinch allspice
1 egg mixed with
   2 Tblsp. bread crumbs
2 Tblsp. yogurt
1 Tblsp. lemon juice

■

Mix all the above together well and chill for 2 hours.
Divide into eight parts and wrap around woden skewers to form kebabs
approximately 6″ long and ½″ thick. Keep chilled until ready to broil.
Cook over broiler (preferabely charcoal) or in the oven. Serve with tabbouleh salad
and rice pilaf. Serves 4.

Anton
&
Michel

Mission between Ocean & 7th, Carmel, California
Reservations: 624-2406

■ ■ ■

Critic's Choice Recipe Collection

BEAU THAI

Neur P'ad Nam Man Hoi
Beef & Broccoli in Oyster Sauce

1 Tblsp. vegetable oil
½ tsp. garlic, chopped
½ cup beef, cut in small bite-size pieces
⅛ cup oyster sauce
10 pieces broccoli (flowers & sliced stem)
¼ tsp. flour

■

Stir fry first three ingredients until beef is pink. Add oyster sauce and broccoli and stir fry for an additional 1½ minutes. Add flour, blend into sauce and serve. Serves 2.

DAVID WALTON'S
BEAU THAI
RESTAURANT

Carmel Plaza, Ocean & Junipero, Carmel, California
Reservations: 626-0191

■ ■ ■

Critic's Choice Recipe Collection

BINDEL'S

Roast Leg of Lamb

½ ea. leg of lamb, boneless	**Pinot Noir Sauce:**
5 oz. feta cheese	3 cups Pinot Noir
¾ cup pistachios	3 oz. port wine
1 lb. spinach, blanched	4 cups demi-glace
kosher salt	1 Tblsp. tapenade
coarse black pepper	(black olive puree)
4 garlic cloves	

■

Trim lamb of any excess fat. Lightly season inside of lamb.

In a food processor coarsely chop pistachios, add feta and blend until mixed, but don't over chop pistachios.

Place a ¼ inch layer of blanched spinach and a ¼ inch layer of feta mixture on the lamb leg.

Roll it up and tie, cut 4 little incisions and push garlic cloves in. Season outside of lamb.

Sear to a nice golden brown and place in a preheated oven of 350° for approximately 40 minutes or until inside temperature reaches 140°.

Pinot Noir Sauce: Reduce Pinot Noir and port wine until only ¼ inch is left in pan. Add demi-glace, reduce to desired consistency and strain. Season with kosher salt and mix in tapenade. Serves 6.

Bindel's

500 Hartnell, Monterey, California
Reservations: 373-3737

■ ■ ■

Critic's Choice Recipe Collection

CENTRAL 159

Beijing Marinade for Pork or Chicken

1 cup unseasoned rice wine vinegar
2 tsp. black bean paste with chilis
1 bunch scallions, topped
  and finely chopped
½ cup dark soy sauce
1 1" piece fresh ginger, peeled
  and finely grated
½ tsp. crushed red chili flakes
4 cloves garlic, minced
1 cup sesame seeds

■

Combine all ingredients EXCEPT sesame seeds in a small mixing bowl and stir. It's best to marinate selected food items in this marinade a minimum of 3-4 hours. After allowing pork or chicken to marinate, roll in the sesame seeds prior to grilling.
Note: Try not to use toasted sesame seeds because they will continue toasting on the grill and can become over-toasted. Serves 8 (3 whole pork loins).

159 Central Avenue, Pacific Grove, California
Reservations: 372-2235

■   ■   ■

Critic's Choice Recipe Collection

CLUB XIX

Roast Loin of Lamb
Crusted with Pistachio over Vine-Ripened Tomato Hash

3 ea. loins of lamb,
   completely trimmed
4 oz. pistachio nuts, ground
⅓ cup dijon mustard
   salt
   ground black peppercorns

Tomato Hash:
4 ea. vine ripened tomatoes
¼ cup virgin olive oil
3 Tblsp. kosher salt
1 Tblsp. red wine vinegar
½ bunch fresh basil
   (finely minced)

■

Blanch tomatoes in boiling water for 10 seconds, strain and shock tomatoes in ice water. Remove tomatoes from ice water and peel. Cut tomatoes widthwise in 3 sections. Lightly squeeze out the seeds. Coarsely chop tomatoes into 1 inch cubes. Pour olive oil, salt, vinegar and basil over tomatoes and cover the mixture in an airtight container for 20 minutes before serving.

Season lamb loins with salt and black pepper. In a cast iron skillet, sear lamb loins on all sides. Remove loins from skillet and brush with dijon mustard and coat with ground pistachio. Roast crusted lamb loins in a 450° oven for 10 minutes or until done. Let the cooked lamb loin rest 5 minutes before slicing.

Ladle tomato hash over the face of the plate, slice 8 pieces per lamb loin and serve 4 slices shingled on each plate. Serves 6.

C L U B
XIX

The Lodge at Pebble Beach, 17 Mile Drive
Reservations: 624-3811

■ ■ ■

Critic's Choice Recipe Collection

CYPRESS ROOM

Veal and Lobster Medallions
with Chive Buerre Blanc

1 veal loin, cleaned
2 8 oz. lobster tails,
   shells removed

Chive Buerrre Blanc
1 cup white wine
2 shallots, diced
1 pint heavy cream
6 oz. whole butter
1 oz. chopped chives
1 32 oz. pot

■

Stuff lobster tails into veal loin, making a hole with a knife or steel, dredge in flour, sear in saute pan and place in oven to roast at 400° for 20-30 minutes. Let the veal loin rest for 5 minutes.

Chive Buerre Blanc: Reduce wine and shallots in pot to half way. Add heavy cream and reduce until it begins to thicken. Add butter to desired consistency and blend to emulsify butter into cream. Add chives for garnish.

Slice veal loin into ½ inch thick slices. Serve 2 slices per person. With this delicate veal/lobster dish I recommend serving rice and sauteed spinach. Serves 6.

THE CYPRESS ROOM ˉ

The Lodge at Pebble Beach, 17 Mile Drive
Reservations: 624-3811

■   ■   ■

Critic's Choice Recipe Collection

DELFINO'S ON THE BAY

Rack of Lamb "Delfino's"

4 racks of lamb (approx, 10–12 oz.)
20 whole cloves garlic
1 oz. olive oil
   salt and black pepper

Mint Sauce:
8 oz. sugar
2 oz. water
2 oz. white vinegar
1 bunch fresh mint

■

Mint Sauce: Mix water and sugar in a sauce pan. Over high heat cook the sugar until it turns a golden color (caramelizing). Pull from heat and let sit on cool surface for 1 minute (this process is done to let the sugar cool off before adding the vinegar). Add the vinegar and place back on heat. Simmer and stir the sauce until smooth (about 30 seconds). Add the mint (not chopped, with stems) and let sit for 30 minutes. Strain the sauce through a sieve and pour into a sauce dish. If sauce is too thick, add a little more vinegar.

Pre-heat oven to 400°, put garlic cloves in a pie pan with the olive oil. Place in oven and roast for 15–20 minutes. When garlic is golden brown remove from oven and set aside to cool.
Trim racks free from all fat and with the tip of a knife make 4–5 little cuts into the loin part. Push a garlic clove into each cut. Season racks with salt and black pepper. In a skillet brown the racks all around and place in roasting pan in the oven (400°). Turn racks over after about 7 minutes and roast for an additional 5–10 minutes. For a medium rare to medium temperature let sit for 2 minutes before slicing.
Serve with roast potatoes and your favorite vegetables. Serves 4.

Monterey Plaza Hotel, 400 Cannery Row, Monterey, California
Reservations: 646-1706

■ ■ ■

Critic's Choice Recipe Collection

DIÁNA

Grecian Lamb

2 racks of lamb, 16 chops
1 quart virgin olive oil
3 Tblsp. dry oregano
½ cup lemon juice
1 cup red wine vinegar
  salt and pepper to taste

■

Day Before: Clean lamb, remove cap and all fat from meat leaving only the thin layer adhering to the meat. Scrape bones clean, separate chops and cut. Place in shallow hotel pan, mix olive oil, oregano, and lemon juice. Pour over chops and place in refrigerator, turning every few hours.

On the BBQ: Heat grill well and clean. Drip lamb chops and place on grill, watching for flames. Do not let flames reach the meat, the flavor is unpleasant. Sprinkle chops with oregano, salt and pepper. When almost done, squeeze one lemon over the meat.

Vinaigrette: Make vinaigrette from the marinade plus vinegar. Whisk well and spoon over chops at the table. Serves 4.

Carmel Plaza, Ocean & Junipero, Carmel, California
Reservations: 626-0191

■   ■   ■

Critic's Choice Recipe Collection

EL COCODRILO

Grilled Flank Steak
with Chipotle Butter

4 8 oz. flank steaks
2 Tblsp. olive oil
   juice of 1 lemon
1 tsp. pepper

Chipotle Butter:
½ lb. butter, whipped
   until stiff and white
1 Tblsp. shallots, minced
1 tsp. garlic, minced
2 Chipotle chiles, canned
   in Adobo sauce
¼ cup cilantro, chopped

■

Set aside the whipped butter. Puree the rest of the ingredients in a food processor and then fold them thoroughly into the whipped butter, making sure they are evenly dispersed. Chill the Chipotle butter in a plastic container, and dispense as needed.

Combine the olive oil and lemon juice. Coat each steak with the mixture, then sprinkle on the pepper. Cook the steaks 3½ to 4 minutes on each side (medium rare), serve garnished with Chipotle butter. Serves 8.

El Cocodrilo

ROTISSERIE and SEAFOOD GRILL

701 Lighthouse Avenue, Pacific Grove, California
Reservations: 655-3311

■ ■ ■

Critic's Choice Recipe Collection

FANDANGO

Individual Rack of Lamb Provencale

1½ lbs. rack of lamb, trimmed
    herbs de Provence
    salt and pepper
    rosemary

Lamb Sauce:
1 Tblsp. butter
1 shallot or small onion,
    chopped
1 large clove garlic
2 Tblsp. flour

½ tsp. tomato paste
1½ cups concentrated
    lamb stock
    pinch of: salt, black pepper,
    thyme, bay leaf, whole
    sweet basil, rosemary
1 oz. white wine
1 oz. red wine
1 oz. cognac
2 pats butter

■

Season rack of lamb with herbs de Provence, salt, pepper, and rosemary. Allow this coating to season the rack overnight. Refrigerate until ready to grill over mesquite or in the oven.

In a heavy saucepan, saute butter, garlic and shallots or onion until translucent. While stirring constantly, add flour to sauteed shallot and garlic and blend over low heat for two minutes. Add tomato paste and cook an additional two minutes. Add lamb stock and whisk until smooth. Combine spices and stir into sauce for ten minutes. Add wine and cook ten minutes more.

Taste sauce for seasonings and adjust to your taste. Add cognac and cook one to two minutes. Remove saucepan from heat, add the two pats of butter and whisk until well blended and sauce has a silky appearance.

Grill rack on very hot fire and then cook on a lower heat to medium rare or desired doneness. If using oven, preheat oven to 475° and cook for 15 minutes. Turn oven to 425° to finish cooking lamb rare, medium rare or well done. Serves 2.

fandango

223 17th Street, Pacific Grove, California
Reservations: 372-3456

■   ■   ■

Critic's Choice Recipe Collection

FIFI'S CAFE & BAKERY

New York Steak du Chef

4 8 oz. New York steaks
8 oz. unsalted butter
1 oz. fresh garlic, chopped
½ cup fresh parsley, chopped
1 cup heavy cream
1 tomato
   salt and pepper to taste

■

Mix butter, garlic and parsley very well. Heat the cream in a saucepan and bring to a boil. Turn the heat to low and add the butter, little by little, until the cream thickens.
Cook the meat however you desire. Pour the sauce over the meat. Garnish with sliced tomato and parsley. Serve with french fries. Serves 4.

Fifi's Cafe
& BAKERY

1188 Forest Avenue, Pacific Grove, California
Reservations: 372-5235

■ ■ ■

Critic's Choice Recipe Collection

FISHWIFE AT ASILOMAR BEACH

Bayou Gumbo

2 lbs. chicken wings
1 lb. Polish sausage
½ lb. crab meat
2 oz. oil
1 stalk celery, chopped
1 green bell pepper, chopped
1 red bell pepper, chopped
½ Tblsp. garlic, minced
2 carrots, diced
½ tsp. crushed chili pepper

1 medium onion, diced
1 Tblsp. salt
½ tsp. pepper
½ tsp. oregano
   pinch of thyme
2½ Tblsp. filé powder
½ cup brown roux
3 quarts rich chicken stock
1 1 lb. can chili sauce
1 tsp. Tabasco sauce

■

In a large stock pot: Heat the oil and saute onion until soft, add spices, stir in roux. Slowly stir in stock, add the chili sauce, bring to a boil to suspend the soup and let the roux cook out. Add the remaining vegetables (bell peppers, carrots, celery, garlic) when the roux is cooked. Add the chicken wings, sausage (chopped), and Tabasco sauce. Cook until the chicken is done. Add the crab before serving. Correct seasoning if necessary. Serves 8-10.

1996 Sunset Drive, Pacific Grove, California
Reservations: 375-7107

■   ■   ■

Critic's Choice Recipe Collection

FRESH CREAM

Sauteed Pork Loin with Fruit Chutney

4 5-6 oz. medallions of pork

Chutney:
2 green apples
2 pears
2 Tblsp. honey
½ cup port wine
1 cinnamon stick
4 whole cloves
5 white peppercorns
    cheesecloth

■

Chutney: Peel, core, quarter, and slice fruit. Place cinnamon, cloves, and peppercorns in cheesecloth. Tie with string to form a pouch. Combine all ingredients in a sauce pot. Simmer slowly over low heat until chutney holds shape and most liquid is gone (about 1 hour). Remove pouch.

Pork Medallions: Season pork medallions with salt and pepper. Brown all sides in vegetable oil. Serve with warm chutney. Serves 4.

100 F Heritage Harbor, Monterey, California
Reservations: 375-9798

■   ■   ■

Critic's Choice Recipe Collection

GERNOT'S VICTORIA HOUSE

Original Austrian Weiner Schnitzel

4 5 oz. veal cutlets from loin or top round
2 whole eggs
    salt, white pepper to taste
1 tsp. finely chopped fresh tarragon
¼ cup flour
1 cup bread crumbs, preferably from sweet
    French bread
1 cup oil
1 lemon

■

Pound veal cutlets until very thin. Salt and pepper the meat and apply tarragon evenly. Beat the eggs in a bowl. Place flour and bread crumbs each in separate plates.
First dip cutlets in flour, then in eggs, last in bread crumbs. Shake off excess flour and crumbs.
Heat oil in frying pan until very hot. Fry cutlets on both sides until golden brown. Take out and place on paper towel.
Brown butter and pour over cutlets. If calorie conscious, leave off butter and serve as is.
Traditional Austrian Schnitzels are served with a combination of salads: green, cucumber, and potato salads. Serves 4.

649 Lighthouse Avenue, Pacific Grove, California
Reservations: 646-1477

■ ■ ■

Critic's Choice Recipe Collection

GREAT WALL

Asparagus Beef in Black Bean Sauce

½ lb. flank steak, sliced ¼" thick, 2" long
½ lb. asparagus spears, sliced 2" long
½ white onion, chopped into large pieces

Black Bean Sauce:
1 tsp. dry black bean paste,
  chopped in small pieces
½ tsp. garlic, minced
1 tsp. corn oil
½ cup chicken broth
⅛ tsp. soy sauce
½ tsp. cornstarch
½ tsp. sugar

■

Stir fry black bean paste and garlic together in oil for one minute. Add soy sauce, chicken broth, sugar and blend together.
Blend cornstarch with 1 tsp. water and eliminate all lumps. Add cornstarch mixture to sauce and thicken for 1 minute.
Add beef, asparagus, and onion and cook for 2 minutes and keep stirring together for an additional 2 minutes. Serve over steamed rice. Serves 1.

長 城

GREAT WALL
CHINESE RESTAURANT

731 A Munras Ave., Monterey, California
Reservations: 372-3637

■　■　■

Critic's Choice Recipe Collection

HIGHLANDS INN

Loin of Lamb
with Fricassee of Baby Artichokes and Potatoes

1	whole Lamb Loin, 6, 5 0z. portions	8	medium size
1	qt. chicken broth or stock		Shiitake mushrooms
2	onions	3	shallots
4	bulbs garlic	3	cloves garlic
1	bunch rosemary	6	Tblsp. butter
24	baby artichokes	1	bunch parsley
16	baby red potatoes		

■

Sauce: Have butcher remove loins from lamb. You will have two pieces of meat each weighing approximately a pound each. Have butcher crack bones into 4-5 smaller pieces. Roast in a heavy-bottom skillet in oven at 400° until golden brown, adding onions and 3 bulbs of garlic, skin-on and cut in half, half way into roasting. Transfer bones and vegetables into heavy-bottomed saucepan, add chicken stock, and reduce by half.

Fricassee: Cut red potatoes into eighths. Place in boiling water and cook until just done, but still firm. Remove from water and drain on towels. Cut stem and outer leaves off baby artichokes and cook in boiling water with a splash of lemon juice until tender (approximately 15 minutes) let cool in liquid. Remove, cut in half, and reserve with cut potatoes. Cut stem of Shiitakes and cut caps in quarters. Peel and slice shallots very thinly. Remove leaves from rosemary.

Salt and pepper lamb. Saute lamb loins in skillet with hot olive oil, and turn over to brown evenly. Roast in oven for 10 minutes at 375° until meat is uniformly pink. Remove from oven, and let meat rest on wire rack for five minutes to allow meat to relax. In a skillet with hot olive oil, saute potatoes and halved baby artichokes until golden brown. Add sliced shallots (half a shallot per lamb loin), and chopped garlic (half a clove per lamb loin), 1 Tablespoon butter and 6 rosemary leaves each, and toss in skillet. Mound potatoe-artichoke mixture in middle of plate. Slice each lamb loin in 4 pieces and arrange medallions around mixture. (Color should be uniform pink.) Arrange 1 ounce of sauce around meat. Sprinkle with chopped parsley. Serves 6.

HIGHLANDS INN

Four Miles South of Carmel on Highway One, Carmel, California
Reservations: 624-3801

■   ■   ■

Critic's Choice Recipe Collection

KIEWEL'S

Grilled Beef Brochettes

2 lbs. Top Sirloin
1 purple onion
1 yellow onion
4 mushrooms
1 red bell pepper
1 green bell pepper
4 10" bamboo skewers

Marinade:
1 cup rice wine vinegar
½ cup sugar
¼ cup salad oil
½ cup sesame oil
1 Tblsp. fresh grated ginger
¾ cup soy sauce
½ Tblsp. dijon mustard

Cut beef into 1½" cubes. Cut vegetables, except mushrooms into 1½-2" cubes. Place beef cubes into marinade and let stand for 10-15 minutes. Place beef and vegetables on skewers, alternating meat and vegetables until skewers are full. Grill over hot coals until beef is done (about 10 minutes for medium). Brush with marinade occasionally while cooking.
Remove from heat and place on plates. Accompany with rice and serve. Serves 4.

100 A Heritage Harbor, Monterey, California
Reservations: 372-6950

■   ■   ■

Critic's Choice Recipe Collection

LA BRASSERIE "Q" POINT OF CARMEL

Filet Mignon Strips Appetizer

3 oz. tenderloin filet, per person
½ oz. Shiitake mushrooms
1 tsp. cornstarch
2 Tblsp. salad oil
1 tsp. butter
1 tsp. parsley
⅓ tsp. ginger
⅓ tsp. green onions
1 tsp. shallots minced
3 cherry tomatoes
3 oz. Bok Choi

Sauce:
6 oz. soy sauce
6 oz. sake
2 oz. sugar
½ tsp. ginger
½ tsp. garlic, minced
½ tsp. Takanogume

■

Coat beef tenderloin with cornstarch. Pan sear beef in oil and butter. Remove beef from the pan. Add Shiitake mushrooms, ginger, garlic, green onions and shallots to pan. Heat over medium flame. Add beef back into the pan. Add 1 tablespoon of sauce. Cook to taste. Top with parsley. Serve with Bok Choi and cherry tomatoes. 15 appetizer servings.

La Brasserie
QPoint
of Carmel

Ocean between Dolores & Lincoln, Carmel, California
Reservations: 624-2569

■ ■ ■

Critic's Choice Recipe Collection

LOS LAURELES RESTAURANT

Roast Loin of Venison
with Cabernet Sauce

4 8 oz. portions of Venison loin

Marinade:
2 cups Cabernet Sauvignon
½ cup extra virgin olive oil
12 black peppercorns
3 bay leaves
2 sprigs of thyme
1 medium yellow onion, chopped

Cabernet Sauce:
2 cups Cabernet Sauvignon
1 onion, diced
1 carrot, diced
1 celery, diced
2 oz. tomato paste
1 oz. sweet butter
2 lbs. Venison or Veal bones

■

Make marinade. Trim venison loin and marinate from 6 to 12 hours.
Make sauce. This can be done a day ahead of time.

Cabernet Sauce: Brown venison bones, place in large sauce pan with 2 cups of Cabernet. Reduce by ½ and add diced onion, carrot and celery. Cover with water, add tomato paste and simmer for 4 hours. Strain and reduce to 1 pint, add a touch of Cabernet and season with salt and white pepper. Finish sauce with fresh sweet butter.

Cooking the Venison: In a saute pan lightly brown venison pieces in olive oil. Remove excess oil and place in a 450° oven for 10 minutes. Remove venison from oven and let stand for 5 minutes. Slice each loin into 6 pieces. Top with Cabernet sauce and serve.

LOS LAURELES

313 West Carmel Valley Road, Carmel Valley, California
Reservations: 659-2233

■ ■ ■

Critic's Choice Recipe Collection

MONTEREY JOE'S

Grilled Rabbit

2 rabbits, whole
4 sprigs rosemary
4 Tblsp. Dijon mustard
4 Tblsp. buttermilk
4 cloves garlic
1 tsp. black pepper

■

Combine all ingredients and marinate rabbits for 24 hours. Rinse and pat dry. Grill over open flame until medium rare. Serve with killer pinot noir. Serves 4.

2149 North Fremont Boulevard, Monterey, California
Reservations: 655-3355

■   ■   ■

Critic's Choice Recipe Collection

OLD BATH HOUSE

Beef Bindel

6 7 oz. pieces of prime beef
   tenderloin center cuts,
   seared off on all sides
6 thin slices of Proscuitto de Parma
1 ½ sheet of puff pastry
1 egg

Duxelle:
2 oz. black forest ham,
   diced small

2 shallots, diced small
¼ lb. Crimini Mushrooms,
   chopped coarse
⅓ cup heavy cream
1 garlic clove, minced
1 oz. Foie Gras
½ oz. pistachios, ground fine
   salt and pepper
   butter

■

Duxelle: Saute shallots and garlic in a little butter. Add mushrooms and ham. Cook until almost all liquid has reduced. Add cream, reduce to a paste, remove from heat. Fold in Foie Gras and pistachios. Season with salt and pepper. Let cool.

Beef Bindel: Roll puff pastry out to approx. 24″ by 18″. Place Proscuitto in rows of 3. Put Duxelle on top of Proscuitto. Place tenderloin on Duxelle and top with a little more Duxelle. Egg wash around each Bindel and cut puff pastry to make a square. Fold corners on opposite sides, then repeat the fold. It should be totally encased and turned over.
To cook, egg wash the tops and put on parchment paper at 375°– 400° oven until golden brown. Serve with a Cabernet sauce. Serves 6.

Old Bath House
R E S T A U R A N T

620 Oceanview Blvd., Pacific Grove, California
Reservations: 375-5195

■   ■   ■

Critic's Choice Recipe Collection

PEPPERS MEXICALI CAFE

Spicy Chile Verde

2 lbs. shoulder pork, trimmed
    and cut into 1 inch cubes
1 large yellow onion, chopped
12 fresh tomatillos, chopped
8 fresh green chiles - roasted,
    peeled, chopped
4 fresh jalapenos, sliced in rounds
6 cloves garlic, minced
    salt as desired
    fresh cilantro for garnish

■

Cook together in a large pot over medium heat until meat is very tender,
approximately 1½ hours. Stir often, add a little water if necessary to maintain a stew
like consistency.
Serve with black beans, rice, and tortillas. Serves 6.

170 Forest Avenue, Pacific Grove, California
Reservations: 373-6892

■ ■ ■

Critic's Choice Recipe Collection

RIO GRILL

Chile Verde Raviolis
with Fresh Tomato Queso Fresco

2 lbs. tomatoes
2 serrano chiles, finely chopped
1 cup chicken stock
2 Tblsp. butter
4 oz. Queso Fresco
   (soft Mexican cheese)
   pinch of oregano
1 tsp. garlic, minced
1 lb. fresh cilantro raviolis

Chile Verde Stuffing:
1 lb. pork loin
3 passila peppers
   salt and pepper

■

Chile Verde Stuffing: Roast covered pork loin in 300° oven until tender, about 2½ hours. When pork is cooled, cut into cubes. Roast passila peppers over open flame. Skin, seed, and dice peppers. Simmer cubed pork and peppers slowly with salt and pepper until flavors meld. Run the mixture through a meat grinder for proper stuffing consistency.

Raviolis: You can either use fresh pasta sheets from a pasta store or make fresh cilantro raviolis from scratch. Take the chile verde mixture and stuff into each ravioli. Cook raviolis for the recommended time and serve with sauce.

Sauce: Peel, seed and dice tomatoes to make a concasse'. Saute ½ cup of concasse' and finely chopped serranos. When warm, add one cup of chicken stock. As it reduces by half and is boiling, add butter, oregano, and garlic. Add the queso fresco (soft white Mexican cheese) and stir into sauce. Serves 4.

Highway One & Rio Road, Carmel, California
Reservations: 625-5436

■   ■   ■

Critic's Choice Recipe Collection

SANDBAR & GRILL

Filet Mignon with Sauteed Prawns

4   8 oz. beef filets
8   oz. beef consomme
    chopped green onions or shallots
    diced tomato
20 medium prawns, cleaned and butterflied
    pinch of arrowroot

■

Charbroil filet to taste. Saute beef consomme, green onions, tomato, and prawns.
Add a pinch of arrowroot to thicken. (Don't overcook prawns). Pour over filet. Serve
with a baked potatoe. Serves 4.

Wharf #2, Monterey, California
Information: 373-2818

■   ■   ■

Critic's Choice Recipe Collection

SANS SOUCI

Entrécote Sauce Marchand du Vin
Ribeye Steak with Wine Merchant Sauce

4 8 oz. ribeye steaks
1 cup dry red wine
3 shallots, minced
3 Tblsp. butter
½ cup brown veal stock
1 tsp. oil

■

In a skillet, sear the ribeye steaks in smoking hot oil. Cook them to the desired point then place on warm plate. Remove excess oil from skillet, add shallots and red wine. Cook until almost all liquid has evaporated. Add veal stock. Reduce again until ½ cup liquid remains. Add butter and whip. Season with salt and pepper. Pour over ribeyes and serve very hot. Serves 4.

Sans Souci

French Cuisine

Lincoln between 5th & 6th Avenue, Carmel, California
Reservations: 624-6220

■ ■ ■

Critic's Choice Recipe Collection

SPADARO'S RISTORANTE

Roasted Pork Tenderloin

10 oz. pork tenderloin
 1 oz. Fontina cheese (imported)
 3 oz. Oyster mushrooms
12 oz. Port wine
    fresh rosemary, to taste

■

Roast pork loins until medium rare. Rub fresh rosemary in before roasting. Saute mushrooms until tender. Add port wine and reduce until thickens. Pour on plate. Slice pork loins into medallions. Grate Fontina cheese on top and serve. Serves 1.

Spadaro's
RISTORANTE

650 Cannery Row, Monterey, California
Reservations: 372-8881

■ ■ ■

Critic's Choice Recipe Collection

TASTE CAFE & BISTRO

Top Sirloin
with Green Peppercorn Sauce

4   8 oz. sirloin steaks
1½ Tblsp. olive oil
2   shallots, finely chopped
3   Tblsp. heavy cream
½   cup brandy or cognac
1   tsp. dijon mustard (optional)

■

Season sirloin steaks with salt and fresh ground white peppercorns.
Saute steaks in the hot oil in a large saute pan over medium heat for 3–5 minutes on each side. Remove steaks onto serving platter.
In the same saute pan, saute shallots. Add brandy or cognac and reduce. Add cream and dijon mustard and simmer, stirring constantly for 3–5 minutes.
Pour sauce over steaks and serve with fresh buttered vegetables or french fries.
Serves 4.

TaSte
CAFE & BISTRO

1199 Forest Avenue, Pacific Grove, California
Reservations: 655-0324

■   ■   ■

Critic's Choice Recipe Collection

THE FABULOUS TOOTS LAGOON

Cajun Style Veal Chops

4 5 oz. veal chops
2 Tblsp. Cajun or blackened pepper spice
2 Tblsp. peanut oil

■

Gently pound veal chops until tender and even in thickness. Next heat a saute pan until very hot over a very high flame. Then bread veal chops in Cajun spice. Add peanut oil to saute pan and carefully add veal chops to pan. Cook on one side for one minute and then turn veal chops over and cook on other side for one minute more. This should cook the chops to medium rare. For chops to be more well done just cook in pan longer. Serves 4.

Dolores Between Ocean & 7th, Carmel, California
Reservations: 625-1915

■   ■   ■

Critic's Choice Recipe Collection

THE TINNERY

Canadian Burger

2 6 oz. beef patties
2 1½ oz. Jack cheese slices
4 1 oz. slices of Canadian Bacon
2 hamburger buns
   lettuce
   onion
   tomatoes

■

Cook hamburgers. Place cheese on Canadian Bacon on top of hamburger and melt under broiler. Place on hamburger buns and garnish with lettuce, onion and tomatoes. Serves 2.

631 Oceanview Boulevard, Pacific Grove, California
Reservations: 646-1040

■   ■   ■

Critic's Choice Recipe Collection

DESSERTS

ANTON & MICHEL

Creme Brulee

1½ cups heavy cream
1½ cups light cream (half & half)
 4 large egg yolks, well beaten
 ⅓ cup sugar
 1 tsp. cornstarch
 1 tsp. vanilla or almond extract
 ½ cup light brown sugar

■

Heat mixture of heavy cream and light cream together slowly until a light skin forms on top. Remove from heat and set aside to cool.
Beat the eggs and add the mixture of sugar and cornstarch gradually while beating constantly. Now add the cream to the mixture very slowly while stirring briskly. At this point, return the custard mixture to the pan and cook it without allowing to boil, until it thickens. As soon as the custard coats a metal spoon, remove it from the heat and stir in the almond or vanilla extract. Pour the mixture into four individual heatproof dishes (souffle cups) and refrigerate overnight.
A couple of hours before the meal, sprinkle the top of the chilled cream with an even layer of brown sugar and place under a broiler preheated to the maximum temperature until the sugar caramelizes. Serves 4.

Anton
&
Michel

Mission Between Ocean & 7th, Carmel, California
Reservations: 624-2406

■ ■ ■

Critic's Choice Recipe Collection

BEAU THAI

P'onlamai Pun
Fresh Fruit Frappe

- 1 whole peeled fruit:
    (banana, orange, lemon,
    peach, apple or other)
    or
- 10 strawberries
- 5 apricots
- ½ cup ice, crushed
- 1 cup milk
- 1 cup water
- 1–3 Tblsp. sugar, granulated
- 1 dash vanilla extract

■

Put fruit in a blender. Add rest of ingredients. When adding milk and water, use more milk with non-citrus fruit less with citrus fruit. When adding sugar, use less with non-citrus, more with citrus fruit, depending on sourness. Blend and serve. Serves 1.

DAVID WALTON'S
BEAU THAI
RESTAURANT

807 Cannery Row, Monterey, California
Reservations: 373-8811

■   ■   ■

Critic's Choice Recipe Collection

BINDEL'S

Apple Flan

1 cup sugar	6 eggs
1/3 cup water	3 egg yolks
1/2 tsp. lemon juice	3 cups apple juice,
1½ cups milk	reduce down to 1½ cups
1¼ cups sugar	1 Tblsp. butter

■

Cook sugar, water and lemon juice until caramelized, pour a thin layer in each 5 oz. ramekin. Put in refrigerator to harden.

Bring milk and ½ of the sugar to a boil. In a separate bowl, mix eggs, egg yolks and the remaining sugar, whip until light and lemony. Add apple juice. Whisk in scalding milk. Lightly butter ramekins. Fill ramekins to the top. Cook in a water bath for approximately 1 hour at 300° or until set. Check with a small knife, it should come out clean if ready.

Refrigerate for 2 hours. To turn out, run a knife along the inside edge, turn over on plate. Hold both the bottom of the ramekin and the plate and shake downward 2 times. Garnish with berries and fresh whipped cream that has a little powered sugar and vanilla added and top with a mint leaf. Serves 8.

Bindel's

500 Hartnell, Monterey, California
Reservations: 373-3737

■　■　■

Critic's Choice Recipe Collection

CENTRAL 159

Lemon Mousse

8 egg yolks
½ cup sugar
3 medium lemons
    (zest and juice)
5 tsp. unflavored gelatine
    dissolved in ½ cup cold water
3 cups whipping cream

■

Combine yolks, sugar, zest and lemon juice in a medium mixing bowl. Whisk over medium heat of direct flame, or over a pot of boiling water, until light and frothy. Dissolve gelatin into ½ cup of water and stir into egg mixture. Whip cream into soft peaks and fold into lemon mixture using soft gentle strokes. Fill ungreased molds of your choice. Allow to set at least 2 hours for best results before serving.
These can be made at least 2 days in advance and will stay fresh in the refrigerator for approximately 4 days. Serves 8.

159 Central Avenue, Pacific Grove, California
Reservations: 372-2235

■   ■   ■

Critic's Choice Recipe Collection

CLUB XIX

Bailey's Irish Creme Brulee

½ quart whipping cream
7 egg yolks
2 oz. sugar
1 vanilla bean
4 oz. Bailey's Irish Cream

■

Slice vanilla bean lengthwise, add to cream and bring mixture to a simmer. Hold.
Mix together egg yolks, sugar and Bailey's Irish Cream. Slowly add hot to cold and
strain. Pour contents into a coffee pitcher and fill 8 oz. ceramic molds. Wipe away
any air bubbles on top.
Place ceramic molds into a 2 inch deep pan and fill with water halfway up the sides
of the ceramic molds. Bake at 350° for 30 to 40 minutes. Custard is done when it sets
and does not move much when shaken. Remove and chill. Serves 6.

C   L   U   B ™

The Lodge at Pebble Beach, 17 Mile Drive
Reservations: 624-3811

■   ■   ■

Critic's Choice Recipe Collection

CYPRESS ROOM

Marquise Au Chocolat

7 oz. unsweetened chocolate, chopped
7 oz. semi-sweet chocolate, chopped
12 oz. unsalted butter, in pieces
7 oz. powdered sugar sifted
10 egg yolks
5 egg whites
5 oz. heavy cream
   9 x 5 loaf pan, buttered with
   parchment paper on bottom

■

Procedure: Melt chocolates and butter over hot water bath. Mix sugar and yolks briefly, just until melted. Whip sugar to soft peaks. Refrigerate. Beat egg whites until stiff but not overbeaten.

Assembly: Fold sugar and yolks into warm chocolate with a whisk. Mix egg whites into mixture with a whisk using a folding motion. You should lose some of the volume of the egg whites to intensify the chocolate flavor. Fold whipped cream into mixture. Pour mixture into prepared loaf pan. Refrigerate overnight. Unmold by dipping in warm water and running a hot knife around edge.

THE CYPRESS ROOM™

The Lodge at Pebble Beach, 17 Mile Drive
Reservations: 624-3811

■ ■ ■

Critic's Choice Recipe Collection

DELFINO'S ON THE BAY

Raspberry Pizza
with Basil Custard Sauce

1 package frozen puff pastry dough
½ lb. Mascarpone cheese
1 cup heavy cream
¼ cup sugar
2 pints raspberries

Basil Custard Sauce:
1 cup heavy cream
¼ cup sugar
3 yolks
1 vanilla bean, split
½ cup fresh basil leaves

■

Cut 4″ rounds out of defrosted puff pastry dough. Make indentation with 3″ cutter to form border. Egg wash pastry and sprinkle with sugar. Bake at 400° for 20 minutes or until pastry is golden brown. Cool and with a knife remove inner circle of pizzas. Whip Mascarpone, heavy cream and sugar together until stiff. Pile onto pizza shell with pastry bag or spread with a knife. Arrange raspberries on top. Serve with basil custard sauce.

Basil Custard Sauce: Bring cream, sugar and vanilla bean to a boil. Remove from heat. Whip yolks, temper with some of hot cream and add to the saucepan. Whisk over low heat until custard coats a spoon. Chill. Remove vanilla bean. In a food processor - process vanilla sauce with basil leaves. Serves 4.

Delfino's
ON THE BAY

Monterey Plaza Hotel, 400 Cannery Row, Monterey, California
Reservations: 646-1706

■   ■   ■

Critic's Choice Recipe Collection

DIÁNA

Baklava

1½ lbs. filo pastry
2½ cups walnuts, crushed
1½ cups almonds, crushed
1½ lbs. butter (sweet, no salt)
10 oz. honey
30 oz. syrup

Syrup:
 boiling water
 granulated sugar
2-3 oz. cinnamon

■

Butter large baking pan. Place your first sheet of filo pastry on buttered pan, then butter the side facing up. Repeat this for 18-20 layers.
Next layer the crushed almonds and walnuts. Continue buttering the layers of filo another 18-20 times. Cut pastry into 30 diagonal pieces. Preheat oven to 375°. Bake until golden brown. Take out of oven and pour the syrup and honey over the Baklava. Let set for 1 to 2 hours. Serves 6.

DIÁNA

Carmel Plaza, Ocean & Junipero, Carmel, California
Reservations: 626-0191

■ ■ ■

Critic's Choice Recipe Collection

EL COCODRILO

Chocolate Truffle Torte

Pie Crust:
2 cups Hydrox or Oreo cookie crumbs
2 oz. butter
1 cup crushed toasted almond slivers

Torte:
10 oz. unsalted butter,
room temperature

½ cup raspberry melba
24 oz. shaved semi-sweet
chocolate
¼ cup Triple Sec
¼ cup raspberry liqueur
2 cups heavy cream
1 cups shaved white
chocolate

■

Pie Crust: Mix cookie crumbs and butter, then add crushed almonds. Press into 2 - 10" spring form pans, or you can make a smaller amount, and use 2 - 9" pie pans.

Torte: Heat the cream in a sauce pan to 180°. NO MORE. Let cool to 120° and add the shaved chocolate slowly, incorporating it into the cream slowly. If the mixture starts to get lumpy, put the pan over a double boiler and continue stirring to keep the temperature even.
After the chocolate is melted in, slowly add the butter, a small piece at a time, until completely incorporated. Blend in the melba sauce, Triple Sec and liqueur. Pour into pie pans. Refrigerate. Garnish with shaved white chocolate. Makes 2 pies.

El Cocodrilo

ROTISSERIE and SEAFOOD GRILL

701 Lighthouse Avenue, Pacific Grove, California
Reservations: 655-3311

■ ■ ■

Critic's Choice Recipe Collection

FANDANGO

Creme Brulee

2 cups heavy cream
1 inch piece of vanilla bean
12 egg yolks
½ cup sugar
¼ cup powdered sugar
6 custard ramekins (1"x4")

■

Combine cream and vanilla bean in a medium saucepan and scald. Do not boil.
Remove from heat.
In a separate bowl, beat egg yolks and slowly blend in the sugar. Adding slowly,
pour the scalded cream into the egg and sugar mixture. Place combined ingredients
in the top of a double boiler and stir over medium heat until the custard thickens
on the back of a wooden spoon.
Pour into custard ramekins and cool to room temperature. Refrigerate until serving
time.
When you are ready to serve, sprinkle the powdered sugar over the custards,
making sure to cover the entire surface evenly. Glaze under broiler, or if available,
with a hot round brulee iron, until the sugar turns medium to medium dark brown.
Serve immediately. Serves 6.

fandango

223 17th Street, Pacific Grove, California
Reservations: 372-3456

■ ■ ■

Critic's Choice Recipe Collection

FRESH CREAM

Lemon Cream Tart

Tart Dough
1 cup & 2 Tblsp. soft butter
¾ cup sugar
2 eggs
3½ cups flour

Lemon Filling
6 eggs
1 cup & 2 Tblsp. sugar
6 Tblsp. heavy cream
6 Tblsp. butter, cubed
¼ cup fresh orange juice
¾ cup fresh lemon juice

■

Tart Dough: Cream together butter and sugar, add eggs one at a time, mix in flour. Roll dough into a round ball, wrap and refrigerate until ready to use. Roll out dough on a well floured surface to less than ¼" thickness. Line a 10" tart pan with dough. Chill 15 minutes to harden dough. Lay 2 pieces of foil in tart shell, fill with with beans or rice to weigh down the foil. Bake at 375° for 15 minutes, remove from oven, remove foil and beans or rice, return back to oven until tart is golden brown, 5-8 minutes.

Lemon Filling: In a heavy bottomed pot, whisk together the eggs, sugar and cream until combined. Next whisk in the orange and lemon juice and butter. Combine well. Heat over low flame; whisking constantly, until mixture will coat the back of a spoon. Pour into prebaked tart shell and bake for 8-10 minutes at 325° or until filling sets. Remove from oven, cool completely before serving. Store covered in refrigerator. Serve with fresh raspberries or blueberries. Serves 12.

100 F Heritage Harbor, Monterey, California
Reservations: 375-9798

■   ■   ■

Critic's Choice Recipe Collection

GERNOT'S VICTORIA HOUSE

Salzburger Nockerl

6 egg whites
3 egg yolks
4 Tblsp. sugar, granulated
3 Tblsp. flour, sifted
½ lemon
1 oz. butter
¼ cup milk
½ cup Melba Sauce (raspberry sauce)
    sprinkling of powdered sugar

■

First, prepare a long ovenproof serving dish or platter, preferably with a ½ inch rim. Brush on the butter and pour in the milk. On oven top bring to a boil, so milk just gently bubbles. Remove and set aside.

Beat egg whites with the sugar until very stiff. Squeeze in the juice from the lemon wedge. Using a wooden spoon, fold in the egg yolks and flour very gently. With a large wooden spoon, scoop the meringue mixture onto platter and form 4 individual peaks like 4 mountain tops.
Bake in preheated oven at 400° for 8 to 10 minutes until golden brown. Sprinkle with sifted powdered sugar and serve immediately with the raspberry or Melba Sauce on the side. The nockerl looks like the snow covered mountain tops of Austria. Serves 4.

649 Lighthouse Avenue, Pacific Grove, California
Reservations: 646-1477

■   ■   ■

Critic's Choice Recipe Collection

GREAT WALL

Fried Bananas

4 bananas, peeled and cut into 2″ pieces
½ cup white flour
¾ cup cornstarch

Sauce:
2¼ cup hot water
¾ cup sugar
1 tsp. cornstarch

■

Mix flour and cornstarch together. Add enough water to mixture until you get a pancake batter consistency. Roll and coat bananas.
Deep fry bananas in corn oil for ten minutes until golden brown. Keep turning while cooking. When cooked, dry off any excess oil.

Sauce: Melt sugar in hot water. Add 1 tsp. of cornstarch which has been mixed with 1 tsp. of water (eliminating lumps) to melted sugar mixture. Coat bananas in sauce, take out of sauce immediately and serve. Serves 4.

長 城

GREAT WALL
CHINESE RESTAURANT

731 A Munras Avenue, Monterey, California
Reservations: 372-3637

■　■　■

Critic's Choice Recipe Collection

HIGHLANDS INN

White Chocolate Mousse

12 oz. white chocolate
3½ oz. egg yolks
 4 oz. eggs
 5 oz. sugar
 1 pt. whipping cream

■

Whip cream, set aside in refrigerator.
Melt white chocolate in a double boiler. Make sure the water in the boiler is at
a simmer because the chocolate is very delicate.
In a mixing bowl, put the yolks and eggs together. Have the whisk attachment
on the machine with the eggs in the bowl and ready to go.
In a sauce pan, put the sugar with 1½ oz. water. Boil with a thermometer until
syrup reaches 248° F. Turn the machine with the whisk onto the highest speed,
slowly pour in the syrup.
Whisk until syrup and egg mix is very light in color and bowl is cooler to
touch. The mix should be very light and fluffy like a sabayon.
Place the chocolate mix in a large bowl. By hand, whisk in whipped cream
gently and slowly to keep the air in the mousse. Serves 6.

HIGHLANDS INN

Four Miles South of Carmel on Highway One, Carmel, California
Reservations: 624-3801

■   ■   ■

Critic's Choice Recipe Collection

KIEWEL'S

Tosea Cake

1 cup whipping cream
2 eggs
1 tsp. vanilla
1½ cups all purpose flour
1 cup sugar
2 tsp. baking powder
½ tsp. salt

Caramel Topping:
⅔ cup butter
2 Tblsp. all purpose flour
2 Tblsp. whipping cream
1½ cups sliced almonds
⅔ cup sugar

Cake: Butter jelly roll pan. In a large bowl whip cream until stiff. Whip in eggs and vanilla.
In a small bowl, stir together flour, sugar, baking powder, and salt. Add dry ingredients to whipped mixture. Beat until smooth. Pour into prepared pan and bake at 350° for 30-40 minutes or until cake tester is clean.

Topping: Melt butter in a saucepan and stir in sugar, almonds, flour and cream. Bring to a boil stirring constantly. Pour hot mixture over hot baked cake. Return cake to oven and bake 15-20 minutes longer until topping bubbles and is golden. Serve warm. Serves 20.

100 A Heritage Harbor, Monterey, California
Reservations: 372-6950

■　■　■

Critic's Choice Recipe Collection

LA BRASSERIE "Q" POINT

Pear Mousse Cake

1 can Bartlett pears
  in heavy syrup
7 oz. Bartlett pears, diced
7 oz. heavy syrup from can
7 oz. milk
3 egg yolks
1½ oz. sugar
¼ oz. gelatin
7 oz. whipped cream (not stiff)
1 oz. pear liqueur
1 8 " springform cake pan
  with 3" sides
  Ladyfingers (enough for 8" pan)

■

Combine milk and pear syrup and bring to a boil. Add egg yolks and sugar to mixture and allow to cool. Mix gelatin with ehough water to dissolve. Add to cooled ingredients and mix well. Strain mixture through a sieve and let stand. Combine whipped cream and pear liqueur with diced pears and add to sieved ingredients abovce. Line pan with Ladyfingers standing side by side around edge. Carefully fill pan with ingredients. Cool in refrigerator for 6 hours. Serves 8.

La Brasserie
QPoint
of Carmel

Ocean between Dolores & Lincoln, Carmel, California
Reservations: 624-2569

■　■　■

Critic's Choice Recipe Collection

LOS LAURELES RESTAURANT

Chocolate Raspberry Terrine

18 oz. semi-sweet chocolate
6 oz. butter
12 yolks
3 egg whites
5 Tblsp. sugar
¾ cup whipped cream
2 Tblsp. sour cream
  fresh raspberries

Chocolate Glaze:
6 oz. bittersweet chocolate
2 oz. liqueur of choice
  (Grand Marnier)
1 oz. unsweetened cocoa
  powder

■

Melt together semi-sweet chocolate and butter. Beat egg yolks and 3 Tblsp. of sugar to mousse-like consistency. Blend together with first ingredients. Whip sour cream with whipped cream until soft peaks form. Blend together with previous ingredients. Whip egg whites until firm and beat 2 Tblsp. sugar into firm egg whites. Fold into mixture.
Layer mixture together (chocolate first) with fresh raspberries ¼" apart in terrine pan coated with buttered wax paper (three complete layers of raspberries). Glaze top, chill, then turn out onto tin foil covered cardboard.

Bittersweet Chocolate Glaze: Melt 6 oz. bittersweet chocolate with liqueur of choice and unsweetened cocoa powder (a little corn syrup gives it gloss & texture) if needed, you can thin a little with cream. Coat well chilled terrine on all sides.

LOS LAURELES

313 W. Carmel Valley Road, Carmel Valley, California
Reservations: 659-2233

■ ■ ■

Critic's Choice Recipe Collection

MONTEREY JOE'S

Zabione

3 eggs
¹/₃ cup sugar
¹/₃ cup sweet Marsala
   splash orange juice
¹/₂ cup whipped cream

■

Combine all ingredients except cream in bowl. Whip over flame with whisk until ribbon stage and chill. Whip cream and fold in with base. Serve over fresh berries. Serves 2.

2149 North Fremont, Monterey, California
Reservations: 655-3355

■   ■   ■

Critic's Choice Recipe Collection

OLD BATH HOUSE

Poached Pears in Crepes
with Caramel Sauce

6 pears (not over ripe)
6 crepes
   caramel sauce
   chardonnay wine
1½ cups sugar
1 cinnamon stick
1 clove

Crepe:
1 cup milk
⅕ cup Grand Marnier

2 eggs
2½ oz. flour
¾ oz. sugar
½ oz. clarified butter

Caramel Sauce:
1½ cup sugar
½ cup water
2 cups heavy cream
3 Tbisp. butter

■

Poached Pears: Peel pears and take out the core. Put in deep pot and barely cover with chardonnay wine. Add sugar, cinnamon stick and clove. Bring to a boil. Using a toothpick check for doneness. The toothpick should go in easily. Remove from heat and let cool.

Crepe: Mix eggs and sugar together. Add flour and mix well. Add milk and Grand Marnier. Add butter before cooking. Using 8″ Teflon pan, pour approximately 1½ oz. of batter going up about ½ the sides (thin coat). Lightly brown each side. Reserve.

Caramel Sauce: Put sugar and water in pot, cook until golden brown. Add cream, boil until sugar and cream combine. Fold in butter.

Place crepe on plate, slice pear and place inside. Warm in oven, then serve with Caramel Sauce. Serves 6.

Old Bath House
R E S T A U R A N T

620 Oceanview Blvd., Pacific Grove, California
Reservations: 375-5195

■ ■ ■

Critic's Choice Recipe Collection

PEPPERS MEXICALI CAFE

Sopapillas

1 packet dry active yeast
¼ cup lukewarm water
⅓ cup melted butter
1½ cups milk
1 egg
⅓ cup sugar
¼ tsp. salt
1 Tblsp. cornmeal
5-6 cups flour

■

In small bowl dissolve yeast in water and set aside.
In large bowl of mixer, beat the egg - add the milk slowly, then add sugar, salt and cornmeal.
Add melted butter, yeast mixture and 2 cups of flour. Mix well, cover and let stand in warm spot for ½ hour. Add 2 more cups of flour using the kneading attachment of mixer (or turn out on floured surface & knead by hand until well mixed).
Cover and let rise again until doubled, add more flour until dough is no longer sticky. Let rise again and refrigerate until ready to use. The dough can be stored wrapped loosely in plastic wrap.
When ready to serve, portion out dough in 1″ balls and roll out on floured surface with rolling pin to about ⅛″ thick circles.
Drop in very hot oil, spooning a little hot oil over the surface. Flip over & brown the other side. The pillows should puff up as they brown. If not, the oil may not be hot enough. It's good to practice on a few.
Serve immediately drizzled with honey, a scoop of ice cream & a sprinkle of cinnamon. Makes approximately 15-20 pillows.

170 Forest Avenue, Pacific Grove, California
Reservations: 373-6892

■   ■   ■

Critic's Choice Recipe Collection

RIO GRILL

Jack Daniels Chocolate Ice Cream

1 cup sugar
3 cups cream
3 cups half and half
½ cup Dutch cocoa powder
9 egg yolks
½ cup Jack Daniels Bourbon

■

In sauce pan combine cream, half and half and Dutch cocoa powder. Slowly whisk to insure there are no lumps. Heat to a simmer. Take off heat.
Whisk together sugar and egg yolks until smooth and sugar is dissolved. Slowly add ⅓ of cream mixture to egg yolks, stirring all the time. Then slowly add yolks and cream to remaining milk, stirring all the time. Return to heat and slowly stir until cream will coat back of spoon. Chill before placing in ice cream freezer. Follow machine directions. Serves 6.

Highway One & Rio Road, Carmel, California
Reservations: 625-5436

■   ■   ■

Critic's Choice Recipe Collection

SANDBAR & GRILL

Deep Fried Ice Cream

½ gallon vanilla ice cream
2 cups bran flakes
   chocolate sauce
   honey
   cinnamon

■

Roll ice cream into balls. Next roll in honey and then into the bran flakes and cinnamon. Refreeze until the ice cream is very hard. Put on a baking sheet in freezer.
Heat oil in large skillet, very hot. Brown ice cream balls quickly. Top with chocolate sauce. Serve immediately. Serves 8.

Wharf #2, Monterey, California
Information: 373-2818

■   ■   ■

Critic's Choice Recipe Collection

SANS SOUCI

Crepes Surprise Au Grand Marnier

4 eggs
1 cup flour (sifted)
1 cup milk
1 pinch sugar

Sauce:
1 oz. Grand Marnier
1 oz. sugar
3 Tblsp. butter
   juice of one orange

■

Crepes: In a bowl, open eggs, add flour and whip until smooth. Add milk and whip again, then add sugar. In a lightly oiled saute pan pour a light film of this batter and cook over medium heat on both sides until brown, Use all of the batter. Then divide crepes among four plates.

Sauce: In the same pan add juice of orange, sugar and Grand Marnier. Boil then add butter. Reduce until sauce is thick. Pour over crepes.
Excellent with fresh fruit and ice cream. Serves 4.

Sans Souci

French Cuisine

Lincoln Between 5th & 6th, Carmel, California
Reservations: 624-6220

■ ■ ■

Critic's Choice Recipe Collection

SPADARO'S RISTORANTE

Tiramisu

     1 bag Ladyfingers
    1½ lbs. Mascarpone cheese
     7 cups espresso coffee
     1 cup Myers Rum
    12 eggs
     3 cups sugar
        grated chocolate

■

Blend eggs, sugar, rum and Mascarpone. Set espresso coffee in bowl on the side and dip Ladyfingers in coffee. Line in a baking dish (approximately 4x10) with Mascarpone. Continue same process until you reach the top of the pan. Let sit overnight. Sprinkle with grated chocolate. Serve next day. Serves 12.

Spadaro's
RISTORANTE

650 Cannery Row, Monterey, California
Reservations: 372-8881

■   ■   ■

Critic's Choice Recipe Collection

TASTE CAFE & BISTRO

Very Lemon Pound Cake
with Fresh Raspberry Sauce

⅓ cup butter, melted
1 cup granulated sugar
3 Tblsp. lemon extract
2 eggs
1½ cup sifted all purpose flour
1 tsp. baking powder
1 tsp. salt
½ cup milk
1½ tsp. grated lemon rind

Lemon Glaze:
¼ cup lemon juice, fresh
½ cup granulated sugar

Raspberry Sauce:
fresh or frozen raspberries
sugar

■

In a large mixing bowl, mix butter one cup sugar and lemon extract. Beat eggs into the butter mixture. Sift together flour, baking powder and salt and add to butter mixture alternating with the milk, beating just enough to blend.
Pour batter into a greased and floured 9x5x3" loaf pan. Bake at 350° for 1 hour or until pick inserted in center comes out clean.
Cool 10 minutes. Remove from pan and while still warm, drizzle lemon glaze over top and into cracks that form while baking. Foil wrap and store 1 day before slicing.

Lemon Glaze: Mix together lemon juice and granulated sugar and heat. Reserve.

Raspberry Sauce: Using fresh or frozen raspberries, blend with sugar to desired sweetness and strain. To serve, slice pound cake ¾" thick and ladle raspberry sauce over half. Yields 1 loaf.

TaSte
CAFE & BISTRO

1199 Forest Avenue, Pacific Grove, California
Reservations: 655-0324

■ ■ ■

Critic's Choice Recipe Collection

THE FABULOUS TOOTS LAGOON

Peach Melba Shortcake

1 pkg. shortcake pastries
1 pint vanilla ice cream
4 whole peaches
½ cup raspberry preserves
2 oz. blackberry brandy
1 cup fresh whip cream

■

Remove pits from peaches. Cut peaches into slices and poach in boiling water with sugar for about 1 minute. Place in refrigerator and chill. In a bowl mix brandy and preserves. Place shortcake pastry in a dish and add vanilla ice cream, chilled peaches, then top with raspberry sauce and brandy mixture. Spoon fresh whip cream on dessert and serve. Serves 6.

Dolores between Ocean & 7th, Carmel, California
Reservations: 625-1915

■   ■   ■

Critic's Choice Recipe Collection

THE TINNERY

Cardinal Strawberries

1 qt. fresh strawberries
¼ cup raspberry jam
2 Tblsp. sugar
¼ cup water
1 Tblsp. kirsch liqueur
¼ cup slivered blanched almonds

∎

Wash and hull the strawberries. Combine the jam, sugar and water in a sauce pan and simmer about 2 minutes. Add kirsch and chill.
Arrange the strawberries in 4 individual serving bowls. Pour chilled raspberry sauce over the fruit and sprinkle with the slivered almonds. Serves 4.

631 Oceanview Blvd., Pacific Grove, California
Reservations: 646-1040

∎　∎　∎

Critic's Choice Recipe Collection

INDEX

ORDER FORM

■ ■ ■

Critic's Choice Recipe Collection

P.O. Box 221881, Carmel, CA 93922
(408) 372-3463

ORDERED BY:

Name
_____

Address
_____

City
_____

State _____ Zip _____

Daytime Phone (In case there is a question about your order.)
(___) _____

SHIP TO: If different from "ordered by"

Name
_____

Address
_____

City
_____

State _____ Zip _____

QUANTITY	UNIT PRICE	TOTAL
_____	$15.95	_____

SUB TOTAL AMOUNT $_____

CA DELIVERY, ADD APPLICABLE SALES TAX $_____

POSTAGE AND HANDLING (SEE CHART) $_____

TOTAL $_____

If you are not completely satisfied, please return within 10 days for a refund (excluding postage & handling).

Make Check or Money Order Payable to: CRITIC'S CHOICE, P.O. Box 221881, Carmel, CA 93922. Please allow 2-3 weeks for delivery.

POSTAGE & HANDLING	
Sub Total Amount	Add
Up to $15.95	$2.95
$15.96 – $31.90	$3.95
$31.91 – $47.85	$4.95
$47.86 – $63.80	$5.95
Over $64.00 please call (408) 372-3463	